Unbreakable

*How to Heal, Transform, and Create
the Life and Business of Your Dreams*

Soribel Martinez, LCSW, MBA

GREEN HEART
LIVING
— PRESS —

Unbreakable: How to Heal, Transform and Create the Life and Business of Your Dreams

ISBN Paperback: 978-1-954493-44-5

ISBN Hardcover: 978-1-954493-46-9

Cover design: Barb Pritchard of Infinity Brand Designs

Cover photo: Leslie Gomez of LMG Photography

Published by Green Heart Living Press

praise for
Unbreakable

"*Unbreakable* takes a deep dive into the journey of a fierce entrepreneurho epitomizes the American Dream! Soribel's vulnerability in sharing her journey and overcoming her obstacles is precisely what every entrepreneur needs to read about being on the road to becoming unbreakable. You are in for an incredible ride with challenging self-evaluations that are practical and simple to follow. Spectacular book!"

Ivy Trevitazzo-Flordelis
Entrepreneur

"Soribel shares relatable stories that many of us experience and tell ourselves, oftentimes limiting our growth. She provides concepts and self-evaluations, prompting deep searching and healing that build resilience. Powerful book! #unbreakable."

Atneciv Rodriguez
Master Certified and Licensed Business Coach,
Executive Leadership LLC

"Soribel's journey is an inspiring story of grit, determination, and glory that will have you turning the pages to see what happens next. Despite many obstacles, her spirit and determination turned failure into success. At every turn, she let doubt become determination and failure fueled her fire, proving to us that despite cultural differences, we are indeed unbreakable. This powerful narrative teaches us that despite our hardships, we can achieve unimaginable feats through grit and resilience. If you're looking for inspiration on your journey to greatness, this book is for you!

Stacey Cohen, CEO, Co-Communications
and Author, *Brand Up: The Ultimate Playbook for College &*
Career Success in the Digital World

"Wow, Wow, Wow! You snagged my heart early in with your story as I read how you got to where you are today. You went through incredible diversity, challenges, and life lessons and could see the light at the end of the tunnel. This book captures your attention with your infectious stories and offers excellent lessons from which we can all learn - a must-read."

Doreen Dilger
Business Coach and Mentor

"I found the book very inspiring, powerful, uplifting, identifiable, motivational, and above all a whole new experience, lessons to take/learn from, powerful message(s) behind it. I loved how incredibly well and descriptive the story was told by the author. Extremely powerful of a young female, her trajectory of life events she experienced from an early age, endured, rose from, and never ever gave up on herself, her dreams, and aspirations, extremely motivational and uplifting. Title of the book is amazing, powerful, eye opener, and representation on the spot!"

Alicia Fernandes
Licensed Master Social Worker

"Soribel is a fantastic woman, therapist, businesswoman, Coach, author, and overall human being! She is a beautiful force to be reckoned with. There are few with her level of energy, integrity, and commitment. *Unbreakable* is much more than a memoir. I'd call the book inspirational personal development. Soribel's stories are every woman's stories - loss, heartbreak, and the pull of societal expectations. Soribel shares stories of how adversity tried time and again to pull her away from her passions and her purpose in life. Combined with her compelling stories, the self-evaluation prompts guide readers on a personal growth journey. Soribel teaches us how to look inward, reconnect with our inner wisdom, and create the life we were meant to live."

Maria Chapman
CEO and Writing Coach

"This book is POWERFUL! An incredible tale of resilience paired with practical strategies makes it the perfect resource for anyone wanting to create their Queendom. Take advantage of discovering what miraculous possibilities await - open up these pages now for total transformation and inspiration. There is power in these pages!"

Melissa Trinci
Entrepreneur & Healer

"*Unbreakable* is the book every left-behind child has been waiting for. It is the guide every woman has been waiting for to start to believe in themselves and the power that they hold within."

Jacqueline Cabrera
Social Service Provider

"Soribel's story is not only inspirational, but it's a roadmap to success. It encourages the readers to take a deeper look into and make them a reality. Could not put it down once I started! Soribel's story resonated with me in so many ways and helped me think more thoughtfully about my life goals. It was beyond encouraging reading all the obstacles Soribel had to go through and where she's at now! Makes me feel like I could be there someday as well."

Andrea Servan
Licensed Clinical Social Worker

Dedication

First and foremost, I dedicate this book to God, my creator, for creating me in such a unique way with so much passion, purpose, and vision in my soul.

To myself for the devotion, commitment, and focus to my vision, dreams, and goals; co-creating the life I desire one step at a time.

To my son John-Anthony for allowing me to be his mami, his guide, teacher, coach, and inspiration. Thank you for choosing me as your mom. I love you!

To Jean-Carlos for fulfilling his purpose in my life. I know our short time had a purpose and a lesson. You were so kind to answer your call. Thank you for choosing me as your mom. I miss you! I love you!

To Mami who supported me unconditionally. You have taught me to value myself, hard work, and commitment to motherhood. I hope that my life and legacy honor all the sacrifices you made.

To my two brothers, Ricardo Jr. and Albizu Martinez. I promised you to always be a great example of perseverance and a model to follow. I hope I have made you proud. I love you!

Acknowledgments

First, I'd like to thank my amazing son, John Anthony, for inspiring me to build a legacy and celebrating every win with me. You are my miracle. A miracle that I prayed for a long time. You were selected to walk this journey with me, and I appreciate you so much. I love you. I hope I make you proud.

I'd also like to thank Mami—without whom, I wouldn't have the time or support I need to build an unbreakable business, write books, or speak at events. Because of the legacy of women in my family, I can accomplish all I have. My purpose and my success are because of you. I hope I make you proud.

To Papi, Ricardo, who taught me many valuable lessons that have shaped me into the woman I am today. You have been one of my biggest teachers.

To G, my son's father. Thank you for being the biggest teacher in my life. Because of some of your decisions, I have become stronger, wiser, smarter, and more committed to the purpose of motherhood. Thank you for the lessons.

Dexton Campbell, thank you for believing in my dreams and for your unwavering support. Your supporting words are always on time. God has used you many times to encourage me and let me know that I can do all the things I want to accomplish.

I'd also like to thank my writing coach, Maria Chapman, for guiding me as I wrote, edited, and cried over this book. Enercida Rodriguez, my assistant and administrative support for JC's PRecious Minds Foundation—thank you for believing in me, loving my vision, and carrying out every single task to perfection.

A Queen needs support to build a Queendom, and I am grateful for all the women in my tribe who helped me achieve this dream, this project and create my vision. You know who you are; I couldn't have done this without each of you.

XO
Soribel

Contents

Introduction

An unbreakable woman heals, transforms herself, and answers the call from her creator to live her purpose and build the life she was created to live.

When people ask me what I do, I don't respond with my career. I don't say I'm a mother, a therapist, an educator, or a coach. Those things are part of what I do, but they don't define me. I live my life on purpose with a lot of passion and a desire to bring change and transformation to the world. My purpose defines me, and I work in alignment with that purpose.

Working in alignment makes prioritizing the things I value easy. I am a mother to a fifteen-year-old young man and an angel in heaven named Jean Carlos. Creating a legacy my son can pass on to the next generation is important to me, and it's one reason for my work. I value my role as a mother, and I work every day to raise a man who sees his mother as a powerful woman with integrity. Motherhood is one of my main purposes—I do it well. But motherhood does not define me.

I am a caretaker for my elderly mother. I value caring for family and loved ones. My parents were not perfect people, and neither am I. We are all doing the best we can with the information we have at the moment. Mami put her entire heart and all her energy into raising my brothers and me. Mami didn't have the resources and support that I enjoy. She could not finish school as a young woman and succumbed to the cultural expectations for women in the Dominican. As a woman her worth was determined by how well she cared for her husband and children and how much she sacrificed. Caring for her now is my way of honoring that energy and putting it back into the Universe. I care for my mother, but being a daughter does not define me.

I am the CEO of SMPyschotherapy and Counseling Services. SMP is a private group practice in Connecticut that offers counseling, psychotherapy, psychiatric care, and medication management to children, adolescents, adults, couples, and families. My practice provides job opportunities to fifteen therapists and two psychiatric nurse practitioners and reaches over 11,000 patients yearly. I am a business owner but running a private practice does not define me.

I am the president and founder of JC's Precious Minds Foundation, a foundation created to honor the memory of my son, Jean Carlos, whom I lost in 2013. The foundation helps single mothers in the Dominican Republic whose children have Down Syndrome, autism spectrum disorders, and other disabilities find resources to help their children thrive. We also assist single moms in returning to school or opening their own businesses—providing resources and tools to build self-sufficiency. I am a philanthropist, but giving does not define me.

I am a woman of faith. I connect with my God through meditation, prayer, journaling, and focusing my attention inward instead of paying attention to the outside world. I don't find God in a church, although many people do. I believe that God is my co-creator. He wants me to have the things I desire, and as long as I do my part, I know I can continue building a rich, beautiful life. I am a faithful woman, and while faith is my guide, it does not define me.

I am a bestselling author. I've contributed to a leadership anthology and created the book you're holding now—a lifelong dream. I am a speaker, a storyteller, and an educator. I am a doctoral candidate studying social work with a specialty in impact leadership in social work administration. I am a licensed clinical psychotherapist, a concierge sex therapist, and a business coach and consultant for other private practice owners who want to grow their businesses. I am all those things, but not one of them defines me.

What do I do? I am a visionary. I visualize a world where women create legacies and understand they are Queens who can build their own Queendom with the right tools, support, and mindset. My mission and my purpose is to ensure that every woman I meet leaves my presence feeling lifted, centered, and like they can build their dreams. Everything I ever needed to be successful existed in me from the beginning, and the same is true for you. I can't wait to see what you create with this one beautiful life.

Introduction

Why I Wrote This Book

I wrote this book for you. I wrote this book because, as women, we must all learn to define ourselves not by what we do for others, but by our purpose in life. We get disconnected from that purpose because of societal pressures and because we want to shower love and care on those we hold dear. It's easy to get lost, and we must constantly work to align with our purpose.

I wrote this book because, in the darkest days of loss, grief, and pain, I needed books like this one to pull me out of despair. I relied on books to teach me how to build the life I wanted. I used books to help counteract the social pressure of a strict religious upbringing. I sought books when I needed to educate myself and move toward the legacy-building that would help me be the woman and mother I wanted. I wrote this book because stories are what unite us as humans.

You have stories, too. Every woman experiences loss, grief, and pain. Every woman wonders if she's good enough—if she deserves what she wants. To succeed, we must rise against the current of social pressure to be givers, to be selfless, and to never ask for more than we're given. I wrote this book to remind you that you are worthy simply because you are. You were created to do amazing, inspiring things. It's possible that somewhere along the way, you forgot what your dreams are, or maybe you forgot how to dream at all. I wrote this book to reconnect women with their purpose so they can work toward alignment in all areas of their lives. I wrote this book because you deserve to have everything you desire.

Something unexpected happened when I began writing this book. I knew I was speaking to you and to every woman who wants to build a dream life, but I found myself entering a phase of healing and transformation in my own life as I dug through stories and pieced together a literary form of my life. Sometimes I laughed; often, I cried. I had to use many of the tools I share with you in this book to help me out of the dirty chair of grief, loss, and pain. Writing this book and fighting through the emotional upheaval it brought taught me again that the concepts and principles in this book work no matter how often you need to revisit them.

Why You Should Read This Book

Every woman should read this book because every woman has experienced storms, trauma, and devastation in their life. We hear these stories often—women broken down by the tiresome patterns of life. However, we need more stories of unbreakable women—the women who rise up after every storm and create beautiful lives. We need to read stories about women like us who've lost children, relationships, careers, family, connections, and most of all, themselves. We get lost because we feel pressured to care for everyone else, fulfill everyone's expectations, and never permit ourselves to pay attention to our wants and desires. We focus so much on perfection that we forget to live in a place of passion. Passion leads to fulfillment. This book will help you find that passion again. This book will help *you* become unbreakable.

How This Book Will Help You

In this book, I share my story and the stories of women I've met through business or as clients. As you read this book, enjoy the stories and find pieces of yourself in each one. Think about the challenges you relate to and know that you aren't alone in the world. Life happens to all of us. Sometimes life is beautiful and enjoyable, and other times it is painful and dark.

Then, use the skills, strategies, and tools shared in each chapter to uncover your purpose, passion, and power to create the life you want. Permit yourself to live with passion and purpose, to throw aside the pressures of society and the people who tell you you aren't enough. Your passion and purpose exist between you and your creator—you don't need other opinions.

As you use the self-evaluation prompts at the end of each chapter, you'll identify what you truly want, drop some of the stories you've been telling yourself that hold you back, visualize the life you desire, and create a plan to bring you from where you are to where you want to be.

Don't skip the in-depth analysis prompts at the end of each chapter—that's where the real work is. You can journal in a notebook, on your computer, or even in the notes app on your phone. It doesn't matter where or how you write your responses. What matters is that you give yourself the gift of time and exploration. Find a way back to yourself. Even when tears start to fall, and you feel like tossing your pen across the room—press on. It's time to build your Queendom.

To start building your dream, I've created a workbook to accompany this book so you can keep all of your responses to the self-evaluation prompts in one place.

Go to this link to download your workbook:
go.becomeunbreakablebook.com/workbook

Part 1

Acculturated Insecurities

Leaving behind everything I knew taught me how to embrace the unknown of the amazing journey ahead of me.

Chapter 1

Leaving Behind the Known
to Discover the Unknown

*The memories of the past are the lens we use to heal the
soul as she awakens into the future.*

I don't remember when he left, but I remember him being gone. I remember an empty home and an empty heart—a feeling that my family was now disjointed. They don't tell you that immigration leaves an emptiness in its wake, destroys families, and makes loneliness creep in until it nearly suffocates you. By the time he left, I'd already lost so many people it felt as if disappearing was part of adulthood. First, Abuelo, Abuela, and several of Papi's siblings. I didn't know that Papi's leaving would set off a spiral of abandonment that would rock my young world and ultimately spark a lifelong dream.

As a child, Papi was my hero. Ricardo Martinez was the manager of a bank in the Dominican Republic and his strong presence punctuated my childhood days. I'd rush home after school to enjoy lunch with Papi, Mami, and my brothers Ricardo Jr. and Albizu, who we called Albi. Then I was off to extracurricular activities or to play in the neighborhood with my best friend, Rita, while he returned to work.

I'd spend the afternoons at volleyball practice and then playing with friends. Rita and I would gather items to cook in my miniature pots and pans. We would and cook rice or whatever Mami let us take from the house over a small fire outside. I'd wait, refusing to eat dinner until he returned home late in the evening.

Papi would sweep into the house in his business suit, looking as sharp as he had when he left that morning— save for a few wrinkles. He'd fold his jacket over a chair, roll his sleeves, and sit. I'd dutifully remove his shoes and socks while he relayed life lessons. Then, together, we'd enjoy the meal Mami prepared. I'd pull my chair as close to his as possible, wanting connection after the daily separation.

We'd sit at the table, my small body pressed against Papi's strength, and share a plate of food. We didn't need to share—there was always plenty to go around—at least in those days. But having a portion of the food from Papi's plate became a comfort before my parents hustled me off to bed in the way of parents desperate for a few moments to connect in the evenings.

These late-night meals with Papi are where I learned about respect and expectations.

"Now remember, when you run off to play with Rita after school, and Mami asks you to be home at seven, she doesn't really mean seven," Papi advised one night over a plate of seafood and rice.

"What does she mean, then?" I popped a shrimp into my mouth, the richness melting over my tongue.

"Well, Princesa, when Mami says 7:00, she really means 6:50."

I cocked my head to the side and raised an eyebrow—suspicious.

"You see, if Mami is calling you home for dinner at seven and you are washed up and ready to join the table at seven, you're demonstrating respect for your Mami's rules and gratitude for the effort she puts into preparing your meals. 6:50 gives you time to be ready to eat."

"Oooohhhhh! And, if I walk a bit slowly, I still won't be late."

"Exactly, Mija. Being on time shows respect."

Each shared plate in our bright, cozy kitchen brought me closer to my Papi, closer to becoming the adult woman who would make me proud. During these meals, when Papi talked about work and the fulfillment he got from managing a business, I decided I would be in charge of a business someday.

At seven years old, as I lay under the stars on a clear evening in Santo Domingo, a dream formed in my mind. I knew I needed to lead. I dreamed of running a business and having a positive impact on the lives of others. It wasn't until ten years later that the dream would solidify in my mind, but it started at that table, with Papi telling what felt like secrets meant just for me. My dream was born in a bright kitchen with a plate of steaming Dominican food, two forks, two hearts, and one meaningful connection with a man who had an incredible combination of intelligence and wisdom—two related things often not present at once.

That's where all dreams are born, I think—in the connection between people, purpose, and passion. For my father, his family was all three. That's why he left.

I don't remember the day he left or the time leading up to it. I don't think I could understand how life would change without my family lunches, late-night dinner talks, and the connection to my most supportive parent. The coming years would bring so much change that my feet never touched the ground long enough to move forward. I was frozen, my life now punctuated by brief visits every four months instead of a nightly ritual. Those visits were never enough to dispel the sadness or chase away the empty place.

When Papi left in 1985, my brothers and I helped Mami pack up our cheerful, cozy home to move into our paternal grandmother's house. She'd left years before, emigrating to Puerto Rico so she could one day bring her adult children, my father, Tio Negro, Tia Claudia, Tia Blanca, and Tia Capi, to Puerto Rico in search of better opportunities for them and her grandbabies. My father and Tio Negro decided to leave Puerto Rico and move to the United States. They desired more employment opportunities, better education, and a safe place to raise their families.

Abuela's house was much bigger, with beautiful, tiled floors and a large bathroom and kitchen. It was also closer to extended family, with the potential to offer my mother support in Papi's absence. I fondly remembered the house and felt a connection to it since Abuela cared for me as a young child when my mother worked. The move was supposed to be good for our family, but it was bittersweet. Without Papi, I couldn't seem to find home.

But for me, a nine-year-old girl with big eyes, lofty dreams, and a love of playing chef with my friends after school, leaving our cozy little house was another loss I had to process without my person. I felt isolated even with the proximity to family members and the plethora of porcelain dolls and toys they showered me with for birthdays and holidays. I lost Papi, Rita, home, and routine, and it would only worsen.

When Papi left the Dominican Republic in 1985, Mami joined a new Pentecostal church. Maybe she felt she needed community and connection while she lived without her partner. The church became another unwelcome change in my life. The congregation was so strict, especially toward women and girls, that wearing pants was now forbidden. I faced having to give up my place on the volleyball team because of the uniforms. Luckily Mami fought for me on that one.

Unfortunately, Mami expected me to follow the rest of the regulations for women and girls. In addition to giving up wearing pants, we couldn't wear makeup or cut our hair. I lost the pleasure of listening to music and going to the movies. I wasn't allowed to visit friends on my own. It felt as if giant pieces of who I was disappeared, leaving a shell of a girl where I used to be. The new regulations confused me, and Mami offered little explanation.

Papi did his best to provide support and connection. He sent money home so we could continue to go to our private school, have the comforts we were accustomed to, and help around the house. He called several times a week to see how we were doing and visited every four months—I don't think he ever missed a visit. I remember the anticipation of his visits bubbling in my chest until I bounced around the way a child does on Christmas Eve when placing a stocking out for Santa's visit.

I don't remember specific details about any visits except that first one. Mami donned a beautiful dress for an intimate wedding ceremony that finally united her and Papi. As a young child, I didn't understand the significance, but I was thrilled about the party, and the ornate wedding cake we devoured. Years later, when I saw my parents' wedding photos in our apartment in Connecticut, I was shocked to see myself in the picture.

"Mami, why am I in your wedding photos?"

Mami took the photo from my hand, "Because you were nine when we married."

"Wait, I thought you were married the whole time."

"No, no."

Mami explained that my father's parents emigrated to Puerto Rico without their adult children, hoping they could bring them to the United States someday. If Papi or his brothers had married, it would have made the immigration process much more difficult. So, Papi's first visit to the Dominican Republic after he emigrated was a wedding for him and Mami.

Keeping to his word, Papi would appear at Abuela's house every few months—strong and steady but a little more distant. It's hard to stay connected to your person when an ocean separates you. There often wasn't time on these visits for long conversations and talks about how my brothers and I were adjusting to life at Abuela's. As the years went by I felt less and less connected to the man I used to share shrimp with.

Without Papi, I was never home. Home was the small house with bright colors, warm kitchen, and Rita down the street. This big, cold house was always Abuela's. I knew Papi was trying to make a better life for us, but I didn't know the details. I didn't know when we'd be able to join him. My parents never explained the details to us. I didn't realize that living at Abuela's was tolerable compared to what came next.

Years later, when Mami left to join Papi in the United States, my brothers and I couldn't go. Immigration laws required my parents to be employed and financially stable to ensure our family wouldn't depend on welfare when we joined them. In 1988 when I was 12 years old, Papi received permission for only Mami to join him in the United States. Though my father possessed a graduate degree in business administration and managed a bank in the Dominican Republic, he could not find equal work in the United States. My father worked days at a meat market while Mami worked as a machine operator. In the evenings, they'd work together cleaning office buildings. My brothers and I would stay in the Dominican with my Tia Anna and Tio Pablo to look after us at Abuela's house. Without Mami, my brothers and I became even more withdrawn and isolated. I'd have taken Mami back— even with all the regulations of her new religion—in a heartbeat.

Since Papi's dream was to build a beautiful life for his family, he continued to send support back to the Dominican Republic. There was money for schooling, clothes, food, housekeepers, and even the pizza and ice cream we enjoyed as occasional treats. But Tia Anna didn't use the money for those things. I'm not sure what she did with it—though my imagination can create plenty of possibilities. But we never saw pizza or ice cream again, and I became the housekeeper.

I'd spend so much time with my hands in soapy water scrubbing laundry without even the assistance of a washing board that my hands were raw and covered in oozing sores. Gone were the plates piled with Mami's fish, lobster, and eggs. Instead, our dinner every night was a ham and cheese sandwich. Mami and Papi—consumed with trying to create a life in the United States so we could join them, never asked how Anna and Pablo treated us. I think they assumed we'd be cared for with the love and compassion of family. Since they didn't ask, we never told them. They didn't visit that year because they wanted to save money and get us to the United States as soon as possible.

I learned to keep the sad things inside. The trouble with that is that no matter how deep you stuff the sadness, the loneliness, and the other bad feelings with no place to go, they eventually seep out. It meant I started wetting the bed at 12 years old—my young nervous system could not process the changes in my life.

My father's sister, Tia Claudia, visited us at Abuela's house shortly after my parents left. "Sori, why do you have blisters on your hands?"

I hid my hands behind my back and blinked hard to keep the tears from rolling down my cheeks. "From the laundry." I choked out.

"What do you mean the laundry?" Tia Claudia looked into my eyes.

"I wash the laundry and the scrubbing—it hurts."

Tia Claudia stormed off to have a word with Anna and Pablo. My parents were sending money for our care—why was I washing laundry with my bare hands?

Tia Claudia noticed the refrigerator was empty, there was no fresh food in the house, and we were doing chores my father was paying for. Claudia went to the grocery store and stocked our fridge. She tried to help to improve our living situation until our parents could return. I wish Tia Claudia's intervention had been successful. Instead, Tia Anna and Tio Pablo moved us far away from the rest of the family into a concrete house with a zinc roof. I can still remember the sound of rain hitting the metal roof—a relentless *plink, plink* that kept me awake at night and shattered the edges of my already raw nerves during long days stuck inside without any of the comforts we were used to. We no longer had running water and had to carry it into the house from a tank. That was the good thing about the rain, I suppose. It meant we'd have enough water collected in the tank for showers.

In our other homes, my brothers and I each had our own room. We now shared a bedroom and had even more chores piled on our small shoulders. All my dolls, our bikes, and even my kitchen with the real pots and pans disappeared. We changed schools again. I lost my recreational activities, I wasn't studying English anymore, and volleyball—which I'd always loved—wasn't part of my life then.

Living with my aunt and uncle, we had no family nearby, no friends, no Mami, and no Papi. Life was gray surroundings, Tia Anna, chores, rice with eggs, and ham sandwiches. My brothers and I, seeking comfort in whatever way we could, found ourselves huddled in the same bed each night despite having our own sleeping spaces. In extreme hardship, connection with others can keep your spirit alive.

After a year, my parents returned to take my brothers and me to the United States. If I was a kid on Christmas in advance of Papi's visits in years prior, I was now a pot overboiling on the stove. The excitement consumed me. When Mami saw how we lived, though, she became distraught. We'd moved from a bright, cozy home to Abuela's big, beautiful one but ended up living without life's basic necessities. Mami ended up hospitalized because she couldn't believe how her babies were living.

We only stayed a few days after my parent's arrival before the five of us made the journey to our new home—Waterbury, Connecticut. We went to my parents' small apartment, then to Pathmark, the supermarket near our new home. My parents gave Ricardo, Albizu, and me our own carts.

"Put anything you want in the cart," they told us.

And we did. I piled my cart with all my favorite snacks and the fresh fruit we'd missed while staying with Tia Anna. After a year of living without the variety of food we were accustomed to, this felt like an incredible gift. I still remember the smell of the first breakfast Mami made in our new home—mashed potatoes and eggs. The days of ham sandwiches were over. I've never eaten a sandwich since.

Our new home was a small apartment on a hilly street in Waterbury, Connecticut, though our father built a house for us later that year. The house was one of my parents' dreams—of which there were many. I knew in my brain that everything we'd been through to get here was part of my parent's dreams for my brothers and me, but that doesn't mean my heart understood. I had my papi and my mami back, but not the warmth of our cozy home. In my imagined post-immigration world, we'd have long lunches again, followed by busy afternoons and ending with a shared plate of food and the warmth of knowing you belong. But that isn't what happened.

My parents worked hard to provide for my brothers and me, meaning they kept long hours. My brothers and I helped with household chores, though most housework fell to me because boys and men weren't expected to cook or clean. I thought that when Papi and I reunited, it would feel like those shared meals in our little kitchen. But, after four long years, Papi and I couldn't find that same rhythm. We had long conversations, and he imparted all the fatherly lessons he thought I'd need to know, but there was something missing. I still loved him, and somewhere inside, I knew I was still his little Princesa, but it seemed impossible that I'd ever feel like I belonged anywhere again.

I especially didn't belong at school.

It was March when we arrived in Connecticut, the spiraling tendrils of winter still gripping the air as they often do in New England. My Dominican-born bones weren't accustomed to the cold, and since my mother still subscribed to the Pentecostal religion, pants were forbidden. I shivered at the bus stop in a skirt, my skinny legs covered in goosebumps and my teeth chattering. I'd climb on the bus and head to North End Middle School while the kids around me hurled spitballs and curses at me, at each other, and our poor bus driver.

In the Dominican, I was a freshman in high school. When I came to the US two-thirds of the way through a school year, they placed me in a seventh-grade bilingual classroom. Being placed backward in school devastated me, and the bilingual program was not the best place to learn English or anything else that mattered. I attended private school in the Dominican Republic with a chauffeur to drive me. I sat in classrooms where children respected teachers as if they were parents—perhaps a bit more. School in Connecticut was nothing like I expected. I dodged insults in the hallways, girls shouting, "hoe" or "bitch" as I hustled past, head down, hoping to avoid the worst of the bullying.

Classrooms weren't much better. Students talked over the teachers and threw things across the room. Life was a misery sundae—one scoop of cold, another of bullying, a third of lost connections topped with an inability to communicate with anyone about the turmoil I experienced. I became withdrawn and shut in my bedroom whenever I wasn't in school. I can't remember what I would do on those long afternoons and weekend days surrounded by my four walls. I remember isolation, tears, and feeling like I'd never again have the happy life I remembered from our cozy home in the Dominican Republic. When Monday morning rolled around, I'd slip on another skirt, trudge to the bus stop, and clench my teeth for another day in my new "home."

When I mentioned the bullying to Papi, he nodded as if he knew exactly what to do. "Princesa, as long as those girls know that what they say makes you sad, they will continue. You have to stand up for yourself. And, if you do, there will be no consequences when you come home. You do what you have to do."

I didn't discuss my feelings or the emptiness spreading inside me, but I heard his words and tucked them away in case I ever needed them. I didn't get up the nerve to do anything more about the constant taunting until the last day of school. Finally, the weather warmed to a point where I no longer shivered in my skirt and ankle socks, and summer vacation was around the corner. That day we had a substitute teacher, and one girl in our class decided to make it her mission to derail the entire lesson. But I was there to learn. I knew my parents left us with Tia Anna and moved to the United States to give us a better education. It was my responsibility to take advantage of my parents' sacrifices and do my best to grab every opportunity that came my way. I took the responsibility seriously.

I had enough and said, "Some of us are here to learn."

She turned her wrath on me, "Shut the fuck up, put your tongue in your ass."

I matched her eye contact, no longer the scared skinny girl looking at the ground, "Come do it yourself."

I walked toward her. I got in her face. I egged her on. I don't remember who threw the first punch, but it doesn't matter. I beat her with everything I had inside me. Anger over the loss of my family, life with my aunt Anna, and the constant bombardment of taunting and harassment I endured at the hands of my classmates. I didn't even get suspended, and Papi kept his word. There were no repercussions at home.

From that day forward, school was a much more pleasant experience. When I returned to school in August, I was no longer the girl who barely spoke English and stayed quiet. I was Sori—and she was nice, but if you messed with her, she would quickly put you in your place. See, I had my connection back— the Papi who dispensed advice like Mami handed out food, and now, I had passion. It would be a few more years before I found my purpose.

Growing up, Papi was my hero, but all heroes are just people—as flawed as the rest of us. Papi's family had a lot of discord and turmoil, which I saw growing up but didn't truly understand until I entered my teen years. The greed of Tia Anna, who kept the money my parents sent for herself. The way no one believed my Tia Claudia when she tried to stand up for us and the many extramarital relationships Papi had throughout his life with Mami all spoke to a deep feeling of unrest. That, combined with what I saw from my classmates, pushed me and clarified my dream of being a leader and business owner. I wanted to heal and find a different way to live so I could pass on a legacy to my children.

Throughout high school, I watched one classmate after another trade her schoolbooks for maternity clothes. I noticed how anger and violence destroyed the lives of others. I wanted better for myself, but more than that, I wanted to help others find a way out of negative patterns so they could build a life they were proud of. So, when I graduated from Wilby High School, I headed for Post University with a scholarship. I had connection, however frayed, I had a purpose, and I had passion. Unsure of how to achieve my goals, I asked God to guide me and show me the path.

Chapter Takeaways

❖ Loss and grief can fuel your drive for success.

❖ We all have insecurities and fears but must build our dreams anyway.

❖ Every adversity you experience brings the seed of growth, change, and success.

❖ Every experience can shape you into the person you were meant to become.

Self-Evaluation Prompts

❖ Identify the childhood experience that created a sense of loss, grief, and trauma in your life.

❖ Identify the people and circumstances that contributed to that experience of loss or trauma.

❖ What meaning did you give to that experience? How has it impacted you in your adult life?

❖ What feelings, thoughts, behaviors, and results have you experienced from that trauma?

❖ How would you like to feel, think, and behave instead? What result would you want to create from that negative experience?

Chapter 2
Discovering Uniqueness

With time I learned that my language insecurities were part of a unique being who overcomes challenges to create the life she was born to live.

That fall, I sat in a lecture hall at Post University, full of the confidence of a teenager who thinks a college scholarship will make life easy. Post was a small school at the time, and my first-year biology class held fifteen students scattered around a lecture hall. The professor asked us to introduce ourselves with our name, major, and one thing we loved to do. As my classmates introduced themselves, I didn't even hear them. I was too busy rehearsing my answer in my mind. Then, the student beside me finished talking, and all the eyes in the room swept toward me.

"I'm Soribel Martinez. I'm majoring in psychology. I love going to the bitch," I announced with a smile.

The class froze. The next person didn't start speaking. Everyone's eyes bounced between the professor and me.

"Um, do you mean the beach?" A student across the room asked, their eyebrows raised.

"Oh, um, yes." I didn't dare repeat the word. I let my gaze fall to my lap, hoping my braids would obscure my face and hide my embarrassment. From that day forward, I used the word ocean instead of beach.

I'd graduated from Wilby High School with a perfect GPA, a college scholarship, and a minimal grasp of English. Because of my age, when my brothers and I joined Mami and Papi in the United States, the school district recommended my parents enroll me in the bilingual program. The administrators assured my parents I would learn both English and Spanish. The reality of those bilingual classrooms, however, was quite different. The constant distraction, the noise, and the way other students seemed driven to derail every lesson meant that I learned very little in either language. Thankfully, I had a solid foundation, and my parents taught me the importance of education. I also had the goal I set for myself at seven driving me. I found joy at school where I could—joining the track and volleyball teams and the Junior ROTC. I was a good student, intent on following the rules and meeting the expectations of adults, so my grades were always good, but grades and learning aren't the same.

College was my first immersive English experience since coming to the United States six years earlier. Spanish dominated the conversation in my classrooms, my home, and social interactions. Suddenly I needed to write papers for English, psychology, and biology classes in English. My brothers' placements in English-speaking classes when we arrived allowed them to learn the language within six months. It would be years before I mastered English well enough to write a paper without my translation dictionary handy.

That first semester I labored for days over assignments that took my friends less than an hour. I poured everything into being a good student. No matter how many hours I spent writing my papers, no matter how many times I used my Spanish-English dictionary to translate each word. My grades plummeted. At the end of the semester, my 1.8 GPA landed me in the dean's office.

He sat behind a desk, arms folded, "You are here on a scholarship, Ms. Martinez. This type of academic performance is not acceptable. You won't keep your scholarship if you cannot demonstrate that you can succeed at university. Is that clear?"

I didn't know how to tell him about my struggle with language. I was so embarrassed that I didn't know enough to pass entry-level courses after six years in the country. I left his office with a new resolve. Failure was not an option. No matter what goal we set for ourselves, we are bound to encounter one obstacle or another along the way. True success isn't found without struggle because it's often in the battle that we find ourselves. When we hit these roadblocks, we have to identify the part of our plan that isn't working. I had plenty of passion and purpose in that first semester but lacked connection. Leaving the safety of high school and my family home meant I needed to find a way to connect in the larger world to people and resources that could help propel me to where I needed to be. I needed to become proficient in English, and it clearly wasn't happening through osmosis. So, I started searching for connections.

My academic advisor became my biggest cheerleader. She told me something inside me spoke to her—that she knew I could succeed. She directed me toward the right courses and the proper assistance. She challenged me to demand more of myself and to believe in myself the way she did. When I broke down because the pressure felt like too much, or wallowed in self-pity over how much harder college was for me than my peers she met me with empathy, but never let me stay in a negative space. Once she asked me what I wanted from her when I graduated.

"I want flowers. Roses are my favorite."

"Then when you graduate, I'll bring you 100 roses," she said before directing back toward my schoolwork and my dream.

I sought friendships with people who spoke only English—forcing myself out of my comfort zone. I went for coffee, talked with them over lunch, and studied for exams. I stayed after class and asked my professors questions until I understood the subject matter and the academic vocabulary necessary to communicate about it. I made sure every professor knew my face. The heads of the biology and psychology departments offered enormous support. They stayed after class and invited me to use all of their available office hours. They knew I was committed and would show up ready to fight for my degrees.

That semester, and every semester after, I lived in the tutoring department seeking help with syntax and grammar so I could put my knowledge into my papers in a way my professors understood. I still labored far longer on assignments than my peers, but this was my journey, not theirs. If it took me all day to complete an assignment, I spent all day on it. If I needed to read a chapter three times to understand it, that's just what I needed to do. When I got assignments back and they were wrong, I redid them until I got them right. There are always people and resources available to support us on our journey to success—I just needed to be brave enough to seek them out.

At the end of that second semester, armed with a GPA of 3.9 and a full scholarship, I added another degree to my workload. The administration fought my decision, but I ultimately convinced them. I had my mind set on medical school, and degrees in psychology and biology would give me the foundation I needed for a career in psychiatry. I'd go on to graduate in four years with two bachelor's degrees, but that doesn't mean the rest of my time at Post University was easy.

Once a place of refuge, home had become a place of chaos, threatening to derail my education at every turn. My father held a masculine view of marriage common in traditional Latino households—he didn't view fidelity as something he needed to maintain. Papi's extramarital affairs and my mother's belief that a woman should not leave caused discord. I could see how my mother hurt, and I couldn't understand why she stayed. She was subservient. She cared for the home and the children and kept her wants and needs to herself. I decided that wasn't going to be my story. I knew I needed to leave that environment.

When the semester ended, I looked for a full-time job. I worked as much as I could that summer, rented a small studio apartment, furnished it as best I could, and created an oasis where I could avoid a house that no longer felt like home. I made my own home—a space where I could rest and recharge but having that place of safety and security came at a cost.

I could go to class, study, and heal in my own space if I took 21 credits a semester while working full-time. I'd attend classes all day. I'd sleep for a few hours in the evening before reporting for work on an overnight shift at the Chase Center. As a counselor for the halfway house, I worked with 25-30 men trying to build a better life for themselves. While the residents slept, I needed to stay alert and on call for any potential problems. Thankfully this job presented the perfect opportunity to study while making a living because I'm not sure I could have managed otherwise.

Somehow, I succeeded with that schedule through graduation and then set my sights on medical school. I thought I could manage medical school like I did my undergraduate degrees: hard work, little sleep, and a whole lot of belief in myself.

I headed for UNIBE School of Medicine, hoping that returning to my roots and a language that felt more like home than English would improve my performance. I still carried my translation dictionary to every class and tutoring session. By that time, the cover had been bent, creased, and taped back together a few times. The Dominican no longer felt like home to me. I'd acculturated to the United States and struggled to fit back into the place of my roots. I was no longer a Dominican. I no longer had connections or friendships. Relatives lay scattered around the globe, and even Rita, my childhood companion, moved away. Feeling out of place, and longing for something that felt more like me, I transferred.

At Saba University School of Medicine, it wasn't the language that became my roadblock. Far from family, in a place that was no longer my home, and with little financial support, the stress suffocated me. Papi helped as much as he could financially, but he was still supporting a family in Connecticut. The demands of studying for exams and keeping up with assignments that still took me twice as long as native English-speaking students meant I had little sleep and even less time for socializing. I pushed myself until my body gave out. Physically sick, financially drained, and desperate for something that felt better—even just a little bit—I returned home to the United States. I'd lost my desire to work in medicine and wanted to focus instead on how people think and feel. I let my family hold me up and see me through medical treatments, and while I recovered, I formulated a new plan. I would still be a business owner, and I would still make a positive impact on others' lives. Instead of medicine, I decided to focus on human psychology.

Quitting medical school was the first time I ever quit anything I thought would advance me toward my goals. In quitting, however, I learned a few things about success. First, success cannot come at the expense of your health—mental or physical. To live without health is not living, no matter how much notoriety or monetary gain you have. Second, some roadblocks aren't meant to be removed. Sometimes a roadblock is there to help you redefine your goals and show you that your true purpose lies on a different path altogether.

To redefine my path, I sought council with the people who supported my dream all along. I talked with Papi who told me that whatever path I chose, I'd achieve anything I set my mind to if I stayed dedicated and worked hard. I met with my advisors from Post University—the people who cheered me on through the drudgery of doing undergraduate degrees while learning English. Then, I looked inward—the most important direction to look when making a decision about your dreams. When you get quiet, block out the external noise and societal pressure you can more clearly hear the direction our Creator is pushing you in. I thought my dream was medical school, but in quitting, I found that my true dream was to help others find what I'd found—a way to break unhealthy family patterns and learn to trust myself. I wanted to guide others to make good decisions for themselves regardless of what others may think.

Years later, I'd sit for a television interview about a murder case. As a licensed mental health professional, I was to give expert opinions about what happened in the case.

The interviewer asked, "Soribel, in your opinion, how did the victim's infidelity impact the emotional state of the murderer?"

I sat, confident in my reply, "When the partner cheats it can cause emotional distress."

I smiled and awaited the next question.

The interviewer froze, "Um, ma'am, we're not allowed to curse on TV."

I didn't understand, "But I didn't curse," I insisted.

We re-recorded that segment. It wasn't until the interviewer asked the question again that it dawned on me. When I said cheat, it came out as shit. Just like the beach came out as bitch in my first-year biology class.

This time, however, I didn't cower, blush, or hide behind my hair. This time I apologized for my mistake and laughed with the interviewer and camera operator.

"You just made my day," the camera operator said before we set up to rerecord.

Sometimes, the thing you see as your biggest struggle, your biggest flaw, can become someone else's inspiration or provide happiness. Now, my accent and the way I speak English are not a hindrance. It's not a problem because I no longer see it as a problem. My accent makes who I am—a successful Latina, which is obvious to anyone who hears me speak. It is a feature of my identity that makes me unique, memorable, and relatable. My fluency in Spanish allows me to reach populations I'd never be able to help if I only spoke English. My biggest roadblock became one of my greatest strengths because I rewrote my story.

We all create stories about who we are, what we're capable of, and what we cannot do. Those stories can either propel us or keep us chained to negative, unhealthy patterns. When we feed the negative stories that tell us we aren't smart enough, pretty enough, or fast enough, they become bigger than our dreams until we forget what it's like to dream at all.

Roadblocks feed the negative narratives we hold about ourselves. If I'd let it, my failures with language in my first year of college could have derailed me completely. I could have been Soribel, an immigrant daughter struggling to make ends meet because she never got comfortable enough with the English language. But I didn't feed that narrative. I pivoted and created a different narrative. I became Soribel, an immigrant daughter with enough grit to pull herself from the brink of failure and enough whimsy to throw a second major on top of a heavy class load just to prove I could.

When I quit medical school, I could have become a quitter. I could have identified with that roadblock so much that I never moved past it. Instead, I reconnected with my people. I looked after myself, and when I was ready, I looked around for another path. Then, I blazed a new trail toward my dream. Successful people don't quit because quitters never win. Quitting is simply a redefining of our objective, a shift in our goals, and a clarifying of our dream.

Both times—when I pivoted and when I quit—began with an awareness. We must step back and recognize the problem. Are we putting too much effort into one area and ignoring another? Are we sacrificing our health for productivity? Are we working in alignment with our purpose or are we off track somehow? Figuring out what keeps you stuck will help you decide on the next right move for you.

Once you've identified the problem, it's time to decide. You can let that insecurity, or that deficit hold you back and define who you get to be, or you can pivot. How do you want to define yourself? How do you want to see yourself? What sort of life do you want to create? If you never decide, you are floating along, letting life happen to you, and you stay stuck in what could have been. Don't let your insecurities define who you are and what you're capable of. What you think about yourself will propel you in one direction or another—stay stuck or chase the dream.

When I quit medical school and announced that I would pursue a master's degree in psychology instead, some people doubted me. I'd already tried a graduate program, which was too complicated, expensive, and stressful. They told me I should just accept my undergraduate degrees and find a decent job. You'll find people like that too. These people are so stuck in their own lives that they can't possibly imagine you staying stuck too. They'll reinforce your insecurities and say you can't, shouldn't, or won't. Those people are not part of your inner circle when you have a dream to chase. You can still love them, but they do not have a right to your dream and vision.

Chapter Takeaways

❖ Insecurities are just roadblocks you must overcome in your journey to success.

❖ The things that make you unique are assets, not hindrances.

❖ More passion and less perfection is the key to success.

❖ Failure is the feedback that helps you realign your path to success.

❖ The struggle through your journey may require another Queen to support you. You have to be willing to receive that support. Your willingness to receive support from others will help you achieve your goals faster.

Self-Evaluation Prompts

❖ What makes you feel insecure?

❖ What experiences, circumstances, and people have contributed to your insecurity?

❖ What power has been given to those experiences, and how does that influence your insecurity today?

❖ What negative conversations do you have with yourself about your insecurity?

❖ What new meaning do you want to give that insecurity instead? What new story would you like to tell yourself?

Part 2

Motherhood: The Journey into Seeds and Purpose

The women before us paved the path toward change, transformation, healing, and greatness. Embracing your purpose honors their legacy.

Chapter 3

The Women Around Me

Every woman needs a hero. Every successful woman has a hero. But some of us have to become the hero of our lives.

Every woman needs a hero. Every successful woman has a hero. For some of us, it's a family member, a mentor, a coach—someone external. Some women are not lucky enough to find a hero in the women around them and have to become their own heroes. Anna Rita Rojas de Martinez, my abuela, was one such woman.

Abuela was my caretaker from infancy because Mami worked. She was the preparer of meals, the washer of laundry, and the fixer of all my biggest problems, from a scraped knee to a lost toy. Each morning of my young life, Abuela would dress me carefully in my school uniform—her princesa needed to be well-turned out. She pressed my khaki skirt into defined creases, daring the Dominican humidity to muss it up. My shirt was tucked in, the front free from blemishes. Tiny white socks folded over just so adorned my ankles. She'd wind my hair into moñitos wrapped with brightly colored bobbles before ushering me to the bus stop. We'd stand close together, her peeling a boiled egg for my breakfast. Because of her, I knew love and adoration. But, Abuela was more than a caretaker—she was a Queen running her Queendom.

Born in Santo Domingo, the daughter of a Dominican and of African descent, Anna Rita would live much of her life as an illiterate citizen of the Dominican Republic. Being illiterate didn't mean Abuela lacked intelligence—she hadn't had the opportunity to learn. After giving birth to five children, Abuela found herself alone and needed to find a way to support them. My abuelo Ricardo Martinez, "Ricardito," emigrated to the United States and stayed as an undocumented person while she built a life in the Dominican. Communication was spotty in the days before email and with limited telephone service, so Abuela often didn't hear from Abuelo for months.

With five small mouths to feed, Abuela decided to break generational patterns and build a legacy to propel her family out of illiterate poverty and into a life of abundance. She began a business raising chickens to sell to local families. Each day she'd slaughter chickens before dunking their carcasses in buckets of hot water. Once she scalded the skin, Abuela would pull every feather out by hand to prepare the bird for sale. The work was hot, and her hands were often covered in burns and calluses. To this day, her hands bear the marks of constant effort. But, that chicken business supported her and her children, even affording them a private school education.

Once Tio Negro, Abuela's oldest son, began school, he taught her to read and write. Tio would bring home lessons from his school day, and each evening he'd sit with Abuela until she learned enough to enroll in nursing classes. After a few courses, Abuela gave injections and treatment for minor medical issues to people in her home. Realizing she needed additional income, she opened a beauty salon in her home where she offered haircare services to women who sometimes traveled quite a distance to see her. This ingenuity allowed her to build her own home and send each of her five children to college. To this day, Abuela grows avocados and other food in her yard to sell. She's always calculating ways to expand earnings and increase her impact on her children's and grandchildren's lives.

By the time I arrived, Abuela's children were grown, successful people creating the lives she dreamed they'd have. I reaped the benefits of her tireless support. When I was only about five or six years old, my relationship with Abuela changed forever. Abuelo had finally received legal status and permission to bring Abuela to the United States. She moved to Puerto Rico without explanation. One day she was there winding my hair into moñitos and packing my lunchbox, and the next, she was thousands of miles and an ocean away. By that time, though, the time I'd spent with her solidified her influence on my life.

Because of Abuela's grit, determination, and entrepreneurial spirit, I grew up in a family of college-educated Dominicans. I knew college was not only an option but the best route to success. I knew women could be independent emotionally, financially, and spiritually. I knew I could build a dream for myself as long as I believed I could. I knew I was cherished, that I was important, and that I was valued just because I was Soribel. Abuela's creativity and love of personal growth would catalyze my growth into a woman. She probably didn't know the impact she was creating for the next generations to follow. She began a legacy that would probably transcend the next five generations. She has paved the path. She has created footprints for the women who came after her to follow.

As I grew up, the other women around me were not the inspiration Abuela was—though, by watching them, I learned more about who I wanted to be. Though she dreamed of being a teacher, Mami didn't graduate high school and didn't see education as an option for her. Her mother passed away when she was young, so instead of going to school, Mami worked and helped care for her younger siblings instead of going to school. Thankfully, Mami knew education was vital for building a better life and worked to ensure her children had the opportunities she didn't. In Mami's view, a woman's role was in the home—caring for a philandering husband and chasing after children. She showed her love through cooking, keeping a home, and never asking for more. Mami wasn't much different than most of the other women around me.

Everywhere I looked, vibrant young girls grew into adulthood and married the first man who gave them attention because they hadn't learned they deserved more than that. When those men strayed or ignored their needs, the women stayed because that's what being a good woman was. These women found their value in their roles—wife, mother, daughter—rather than in their being. The women I saw around me as a child were not happy like Abuela. Abuela bustled about her beauty shop with joyful pride because she knew she and her children broke generational patterns. The other women around me didn't seem happy or fulfilled—content, maybe—but only because they didn't dream of more for themselves. They'd given up their right to have a self because that's how they were accepted and loved. Watching Mami, I learned how to care for a household, but I also saw the things I didn't want.

Mami excelled at showing her love through household tasks, but she could not provide emotional support and affection. I wanted to be able to give my future children both. I decided I wouldn't be dependent on a man—if I entered a relationship or stayed in one, it was because I wanted to. I decided that education was my best route to that independence and that owning a business and leading others was my destiny. I decided that I would not live a selfless existence—that I would embrace the process of creating a self that societal expectations and cultural patterns could not overshadow. I wanted to challenge all the limiting beliefs about what women are capable of.

When you're a Queen building a legacy of success and growth, you will need support and inspiration from other women. Sometimes, however, you must piece it together on an assembly line of inspiration—recognizing what you want to keep from each of the influential women in your life and finding those who will be part of your life but not your dream-building team. After Abuela left, I went years without a positive female role model. It wasn't until I arrived at Post University that I'd meet the women who would help me take the inspiration from Abuela and turn it into a concrete plan.

I was fortunate to meet the type of women who would be my tireless supporter on my journey early in my college career. Lisa Kaplan, Ph.D., the head of the biology department, became in integral piece of my support team. After that first semester, where I crashed and nearly burned because of my lack of English proficiency, Dr. Kaplan made it clear that she believed in my potential and that she'd do anything to help me reach it. She'd arrive to class each day dressed simply with her hair pulled back in a ponytail. Her croc-clad feet beat a path in the front of the room during her lectures. She possessed an ever-present smile and always held a mug of coffee or tea. When I finally got over the idea that I could do college the same way I'd done high school—without support—she was one of the first professors I reached out to. Dr. Kaplan stayed after class with me and met me on weekends to painstakingly review the material until her cup grew cold, but her smile never faltered. Her support and belief in me helped me grow into a student whose capabilities matched my determination.

The more I learned about Dr. Kaplan, the more I designed my dream to be a Soribel-specific version of her. She was a brilliant, independent Queen building her Queendom in such a way that her purpose was clear. Dr. Kaplan's passion for science and an unwavering commitment to supporting students showed through every day. She continued to encourage me after graduation, proving that she was invested in helping students develop their dreams, not just in getting them through university. After leaving medical school, I found myself again in Dr. Kaplan's office, feeling bruised and knocked off course.

"What do you do when you hit traffic on your way into New York City? Do you give up on your goal and drive back home? No, you look for a different route to your destination," she said.

So, that's what I did. Dr. Kaplan helped me re-create a plan and checked in via email occasionally to see how I was doing in my master's program and the early days of my career. If you look around at the women who've done what you want to do—who've managed to shake off the shackles of societal expectations about women's roles—they will be glad to lend you a hand, a listening ear, or a bit of wisdom. Be brave enough to ask. A woman who has the courage to ask for what she desires always gets what she is looking for. When I needed or desired help or support, I was never afraid to do so.

Another type of woman you'll encounter appear successful and have a life similar to the one you envision for yourself, but who got there by scaling walls they have no interest in helping others climb. Not all successful women in positions of power will be your cheerleaders while you build your Queendom. The trick is to quickly identify the ones who won't and give them a swift exit from your inner circle.

When I worked as a school social worker before starting SMPsychotherapy, I met a woman I'll call Brooke. She was a school principal, ran a tight ship, and appeared successful. Upon further inspection, however, it became clear that she was not an ally I could rely on for support.

At the beginning of the school year, I passed my licensing exams, allowing me to start a private practice. I planned to start part-time while keeping my job with benefits. I figured that, eventually, I'd have a large caseload to support a full-time therapy practice. I'd leave the comfort of a steady paycheck. I programmed my phone to alert me of my success.

"Congratulations, Soribel! You published your first book!" would pop up on my screen as I brushed my teeth.

"Wow, Soribel! You've got a long waitlist!" would show up on my screen when I sipped my coffee at my desk each morning.

"I'm grateful to run a successful business," would pop up to keep me going mid-morning.

One day, as I sat in Brooke's office for a meeting, my phone chimed, and "Congratulations, Soribel, tomorrow is your last day working in the schools" flashed across my screen.

Brooke laughed, "That's impossible—you quitting," she said, though she knew I'd started seeing clients.

I snatched my phone off the desk and sat back in my seat, "All you have to do is sit and watch. It's happening," I said.

Within a month, I started seeing what my business could be. My waitlist spilled over just as I'd envisioned. I knew I could have an enormous impact on the lives of others. I drafted my resignation letter and handed it to Brooke the following day. "You weren't kidding. You couldn't wait to get out of here," Brooke laughed. I walked out of her office with my shoulders back, and my head held just a little higher. Before I made it to my office just down the hall, my phone rang. The city's human resources department wanted to know what they could do to keep me. A bilingual school social worker in a district where more than half the students speak Spanish was quite the commodity.

"This isn't about the money or the perks," I said, "It's about passion and purpose. This is about something greater than myself."

I walked out of that school building for the last time. I was a business owner. SMPsychotherapy and Counseling Services became a therapy practice that provides quality mental health care services to thousands of people. Brooke didn't get invited into my inner circle.

When you meet the women whose judgment and limiting beliefs attempt to derail you from your purpose, you must hold fast to what you know. Your purpose is born within you. It's the path you walk with your Creator, so you know it's the right one. Sometimes these people will hold a place in your life. They're your bosses, your family members, the mothers you meet in the PTA, or colleagues who serve a purpose in creating your dream. These people are not invited to your inner circle because they will poison it with negativity. You can converse, collaborate, and spend time with them, but don't share the depths of your dream—they can't see it because something is holding them back from creating their own. Not everyone is meant to be part of your vision. Your dream is precious; guard it carefully.

There is another type of woman you'll encounter on your journey. This person cannot see your entire vision, nor are they harmful. Their presence in your circle will not derail you—it may make certain parts easier. They are women who can give what they're able to as long as you remain grateful for what they offer without expecting them to be something they aren't.

Mami isn't well educated, though she finished her GED after she and Papi came to the United States. Unable to become a teacher, Mami made motherhood her purpose—creating a home and raising her children. The women around her were selfless wives and mothers—and that's what she became. As part of being a great mother, Mami has been a constant supportive presence throughout my entrepreneurial journey. She offers support at home, and encourages me in the mothering of my son.

During my journey to motherhood, she celebrated the ups and cried through the struggles. She congratulates me on the young man my son has become and ensures that my home runs well while I'm out building my Queendom. Though Mami cannot be every support I need, I could not create the legacy I hope to develop without her unending love and care. My job is to remain grateful for all she gives me and understand that I can find other support elsewhere.

I find the rest of the support I need in champions like Dr. Kaplan, inspiring people like Abuela, and the business coaches and leaders who've offered their wisdom. If you look, you'll find plenty of support for your dream. In my journey, I often turn to books by powerful leaders and those in the personal development realm. I read accounts of those creating a legacy to gather inspiration. You can also find the support you need if you look hard enough. Seek self-development through reading and learning. Read books by people who have done the things you want to do, take courses to advance your goals, and engage in constant growth. Seek relationships with women who have their own vision because those are the ones who will be able to see yours.

Chapter Takeaways

❖ Every woman needs a hero, but sometimes you have to become your own.

❖ Be yourself. The other options are taken and boring.

❖ Surround yourself with women who have your best interests at heart.

❖ Seek support from women around you who are worth listening to.

❖ A Queen must have support to create her QUEENDOM.

Self-Evaluation Prompts

❖ Identify the heroes around you who've impacted your life in a positive way.

❖ Identify how you feel when you're around these women. How do they contribute to your mindset?

❖ If you can't identify a hero in your life, what qualities would you want them to have? How would you want them to behave? How would you like to feel around them? What kind of results would they have in your own life that you want in yours?

❖ Identify two support systems you need today to help you in your journey. Where might you find that support?

Chapter 4

Miracles and Birthing of Life and New Purpose

*Every loss in life brings within it a seed of purpose
and births new opportunity.*

My fiancé and I sat in the specialist's office, fingers laced together, pouring out the details of our dream of parenthood to a stranger across the desk. When you're a woman struggling to get pregnant, it can feel like your body is broken or at least non-compliant. You're supposed to be able to bring new life into the world, but something keeps going wrong. At that point, we'd celebrated a positive pregnancy test three times only to have our hopes dashed a few months later when ultrasounds and the familiar cramping revealed that, yet again, my body didn't do its job.

I sat, detailing these losses to a doctor who felt like my only hope. For months we'd tracked my ovulation. I'd call G while he was at work to let him know he needed to be home immediately after his shift at the hospital so we could get down to business. We'd entered that space so many couples who struggle with fertility find themselves in where sex becomes a means to an end instead of the destination. But, each month, my period started like clockwork, and my dream of becoming a mother felt further away.

"Before we talk about your options, let's do a physical exam and ensure everything is working as it should," the doctor said, closing my file on his desk.

In the exam room, exposed in a flimsy gown, I lifted my feet into stirrups thinking of all the times I'd done this and learned that my baby didn't make it. I thought of the years I spent trying not to get pregnant and how strange that our goals change depending on the season of life we move through.

"Well, it seems you won't need my services after all," the doctor said, a slight smile on his face.

"What do you mean?" I asked, trying to sit up as best I could with my feet still in the stirrups.

"It appears that you are already pregnant."

G and I locked eyes, elated at the possibilities and terri-fied of another loss. Miscarriage does that—it steals the fantasy of pregnancy from women and replaces it with an intense fear that this pregnancy will end the same way as the others.

"So, let's see what we can do to ensure this pregnancy sticks, shall we?" The doctor was determined to help G and I achieve our dream.

Blood tests revealed that my body wasn't producing enough progesterone to support a healthy pregnancy. The fix for that was easy enough. I just had to insert a progesterone sup-pository daily and deal with the messy discharge for four months. Easy, just like checking my temperature, peeing on an endless supply of sticks, and voluntarily being poked and prod-ded by doctors. I was thrilled to do anything necessary to be-come a mother.

G and I lived together in a cozy house and created a nursery for the child growing inside me. Decorating with a Win-nie the Pooh theme, building furniture, and sitting in the rock-ing chair became a way for me to celebrate this pregnancy and continue to be healthy. I exerted control where I could. I read every book about pregnancy I could find. I took labor classes and breastfeeding classes. I ate only organic food, gave up cof-fee, limited my sugar intake, and exercised. If going to Zumba made me more likely to deliver a healthy baby, I was willing to shake my growing shape around a gym floor a few times a week.

Pregnancy isn't really nine months. Forty weeks is ten months any way you slice it. I felt every one of those weeks thanks to a never-ending morning sickness. It seemed to be my body's way of reminding me I was still pregnant at every mo-ment. Feeling sick made me tired, and I'd spend my lunch breaks at work curled up in the bathroom napping.

Each day G worked at a hospital in New York City. He'd leave the house at the same time and return each evening to rub my belly. During our time at home, G and I read and sang to the child growing inside me. G belted out the song "Antonio" in Ital-ian, and I read all of my favorite picture books. We nested, nour-ished, and prayed that our baby would enter the world healthy, happy, and whole.

At seven months pregnant, I squeezed my belly behind our dining table to pay bills. When I logged into G's credit card account, the balance seemed much higher than typical, and a few charges captured my attention. It seemed G was paying for someone else's lunch at the hospital cafeteria. Upset and in disbelief, I called his mother. She confirmed that he was seeing a nurse at the hospital, which is how he could manage to step out but keep his schedule consistent. When he came home, I confronted him. G denied the affair, but in my heart, I knew.

Suddenly I had to ask myself what choice I could make that supported the life I wanted to live and the woman I wanted to become. I'd grown up seeing Mami and countless other women take back their partners even when one affair after another eroded trust and changed the dynamic of their relationships. I saw women let the fear of single parenthood keep them chained to men who didn't value them. I saw these women allow their self-worth to degrade as they clung to a relationship that didn't honor their worth.

I decided I would have a different story. I asked G to move out and decided that I'd create a healthy home for my baby on my own. My hormones and emotions were all over the place, but I returned to the things I knew that worked to bring me peace and keep me focused on my purpose. I cared for myself with nourishing food and time with the people I knew would support me the most. I felt peace because moving forward as a single parent fit what I knew to be the truth for me. When I turned inward and connected with myself and my Creator, I knew I could not stay in a relationship with a man who didn't see monogamy as important.

After a breakup, there's a pull to sit and wallow in the negative feelings. When you're the victim of infidelity, you wonder if you're the reason they strayed and why you couldn't be enough for them. Such thoughts are common, but they aren't helpful. I felt the pull to sit in that filth-covered, piss-soaked chair of negativity and focus on the turmoil and all the bad things happening around me. We have the decision to make when we're sitting in the chair and filth is seeping around our hips, creeping into our pores. We can continue to sit in filth, or we can rise up, clean ourselves off, and move forward.

If I stayed in that dirty chair, I'd miss the joy of becoming a mother. I'd lose out on cherishing the last moments of my pregnancy, the embrace of a community that comes from sharing your journey to motherhood with the women around you, and the thrill of holding my baby boy for the first time. So, I rose up. I turned to the tools that helped center and realign me with my purpose. I reconnected with God and journaled to get the negativity out and practice gratitude. I exercised my body to celebrate the ways it can move. I visualized the future I wanted to create for my son and me. I meditated and refocused my brain on my truth. I am Soribel. I am a woman. I am a healer. I am a Dominican-American Goddess. I am a mother. I am a leader. Nothing about who I am necessitates having a partner.

As is typical of babies, John Anthony didn't follow our plan for his birth. On Memorial Day weekend in 2007, labor began, though we had a c-section scheduled for a week later. I went to the hospital, where they administered medication to stop the labor and give his tiny lungs more time to grow. But my boy was insistent, and the next day, my water broke, and labor began in earnest. At the time, G was in New York City, and after we let him know the baby was on his way, he began the drive only to sit in holiday weekend traffic crossing the George Washington Bridge. I welcomed John Anthony into the world with my mother beside me.

I caressed his cheeks while he nursed and felt my heart swell. I stared at him as he slept, his tiny bow-shaped mouth wiggling as he dreamed. I delighted in his first smiles, the tender way he grabbed my fingers, and the way his eyes locked onto mine when we rocked. Babies don't really give anything back— they're giant puddles of neediness, crying, and tiny feet. But when you become a mother, you realize that real love doesn't require a return on investment. Real love is midnight feedings and buying more diapers. Real love is retiring home several times a day when I worked for a home-care agency to nurse my son who didn't like bottles. Real love will push you to your limits and teach you to embrace the joy of the tiny, quiet moments.

Though I vowed to embrace single parenthood and create a loving home for my son, shame and insecurity about my choice haunted me. Family members and friends cautioned me that the little boy growing inside me needed his father to grow into a strong, successful Black man—that ending my relationship would cause him to turn to a life of drugs or gangs like so many other young Black men. When I heard these words of caution, it activated shame inside me because the truth was I did want my child to grow up in a two-parent household as I did. The life I was building was a detour from my vision, and that detour was hard to swallow. I struggled with feeling like I couldn't be enough for John Anthony alone. I grieved the loss of a relationship with G and the evaporation of the dreams we shared. In times of struggle, however, the voices you choose to listen to can impact your self-talk and change your reality. I decided I needed a different voice.

I reached out to my supervisor at work—a woman with abundant wisdom about parenthood and life. I'd heard enough of her interactions with her own children to know she was the type of mother I hoped to be. I knew she'd have words of wisdom and would speak a truth that would make it straight to my heart. I asked her if she thought I could be enough to raise a Black man who knew how to stand on his own, care for others, and impact the world.

"Look at the woman he has in his life. Look at how you care for him. Of course, you're enough." She sat next to me, her petite frame contrasting with her knowledge.

She showed me research about children raised with one loving, consistent parent finding success. Two parents did not guarantee success for a child. They needed love and consistency—those were two things I could offer in spades. I continued to stop at home to nurse John Anthony, who spent my workdays with Mami. She took her new role as Abuela seriously and doted on my little man so I could continue working and building toward my dream of helping others create the lives they wanted.

I had to let go of my fear and step into my power, knowing that as long as I worked in alignment with my purpose and stayed true to who I am, I would reach my destination. A woman who walks with God as her co-creator will always succeed. When you struggle, and doubt and shame threaten to derail you, turning inward will save you. Meditate, journal, and ask the Universe to show you the next step, the right path to walk, and the people around you who will be your support. When you connect with your life purpose, you understand that you are part of something bigger than yourself—you know you can have an impact on the world through your leadership, your family life, your professional achievements, your words, and the way you move through the world encouraging other Queens to do the same. It's easy to let societal pressure and worry take over and make you forget your purpose, so we have to build a toolbox for reconnection to help ground us.

When you struggle, identify your dirty chair. Are you overcome by imposter syndrome telling you you aren't enough to achieve your dream? Is there a societal message telling you you cannot be both a mother and a successful business owner? Are you worried you won't succeed because no one in your family has? Identify your dirty chair.

Then, pay attention to the feelings that come up. Observe them, but don't judge yourself for having them, and don't feed them with a hamster wheel of self-hate. If you're angry, sad, or embarrassed, those are only clues for what you need to change when you decide to rise out of the dirty chair. Then, decide how long you want to sit and allow the filth to sink into your skin. Do you want to leap up immediately, or are you comfortable sitting long enough to let the negativity become part of who you are? Do you want to give in to the same monster who lives under the chair, waiting to swallow your dreams? If you're like me, you'll want a plan for standing up and cleaning off as soon as possible. You have too many goals to crush and too many lives to impact.

Once you decide to rise, you'll need to take out your toolbox. What are your strategies for reconnecting with your purpose? If you don't have any, it's time to try a few to see what works. Many successful women I know read inspiring books to reconnect with their purpose and find inspiration when they find it lacking. Journaling about your feelings, goals, and what changes you need to make to align with your purpose may help. If you have a mentor, reach out to them for a chat. As you use each strategy, you'll peel off a layer of dirt, and the shame monster will lose its hold on you. Then, once you've exhausted your toolbox and identified the next steps that align with your purpose, you're ready to return to your path.

That doesn't mean fear will magically dissipate. Even knowing a decision is right doesn't make it easy. When I decided to become a single parent, I knew the road I set for myself was more difficult than accepting a sub-par relationship and having help raising a son. But staying in that relationship would have derailed me from my true purpose in life. To stay, I would have needed to make myself smaller—to give up pieces of me one at a time until I forgot who Soribel was and who she was meant to be. That choice was unacceptable, so I picked the more difficult path. I chose the worthy people around me to accompany me along the way, and I continued building my Queendom.

Chapter Takeaways

❖ Miracles are real and are always happening around us. God is always doing his part and working in our favor.

❖ A woman who walks with God will always reach her destination.

❖ You are worthy of love. You are blessed with abundance. You can deeply and completely accept yourself.

❖ Single parenthood shouldn't be a cause of shame but, instead, can be a source of pride.

❖ Your greatest blessings and gifts may come from the least expected places.

❖ You'll miss the joy if you spend too much time in the dirty chair.

Self-Evaluation Prompts

❖ What is your "dirty chair"? What bad situation or feelings are you sitting in?

❖ Identify the thoughts, feelings, and situations that keep you in the dirty chair.

❖ What are the main feelings and thoughts keeping you in the dirty chair? Observe those thoughts and feelings and release them without judging yourself.

❖ How do you want to feel and think about this situation instead?

❖ Reprogram your mind. Create a new perception of the situation. Identify the tools and strategies you can use to create a new belief system about your situation.

Chapter 5

Grief & Loss

Grief is like the ocean—it can have big, medium, or small waves, and sometimes it's calm. Honor your grief and feel the feelings it brings to your life in any given moment.

Two days after Christmas in 2013, John Anthony sat next to me in an ultrasound room, a book open on his lap while the technician squirted gel on my swollen belly. Thirty-six weeks into a high-risk pregnancy, ultrasounds became a routine part of our lives. This was the second one this week. I closed my eyes, reclined back, and waited for the whoosh of the baby's heartbeat. I felt the wand touch my skin, and the coldness of the gel spread as the technician moved the wand around.

"Why can't I hear the heartbeat?" I asked, struggling to see the screen.

The technician angled the screen away, "Hold on, I'm just searching for it."

"But I always hear it right away. What's wrong? What's going on?" Panic crept into my voice.

"Calm down. I'm just going to get the doctor. Hang tight for a second." The technician set his wand down and exited the room.

I'm not sure why anyone would tell a pregnant woman in that position to calm down. The phrase did nothing to soothe my nerves. I glanced over at John Anthony, mouthing the words to his picture book, then laid my head back down and prayed.

After what seemed like an eternity, the doctor entered the room. He glanced toward me, but our eyes didn't meet. He grabbed the wand and resumed the search.

"I'm so sorry, Ms. Martinez. There's no heartbeat. Your baby is gone." Tears clouded his eyes.

My scream echoed through the hallways of Danbury Hospital. I screamed in disbelief, in anger, and in despair. I screamed for the dreams I had of mothering another tiny being.

I screamed for the dreams John Anthony had of being a big brother.

Another doctor joined the first, "I don't know what happened. Your baby was active and healthy three days ago, with a strong heartbeat. Did you fall or get into an altercation?"

I shook my head.

The doctors' tears fell from their eyes. "Sometimes we don't know why this happens," one said.

Their platitudes didn't penetrate my grief. I wailed, tears cascading down my cheeks until a nurse placed her hands on my arm and directed me to look at John Anthony.

"Look at your son," she said.

John Anthony sat in the same chair as before, his book discarded on the floor. He stared at me wide-eyed—the very definition of fear.

"You are scaring him. You need to pull yourself together. I know you're grieving, but you have a son here who needs you to be strong." She was kind but firm.

That was the push I needed. I stopped wailing and started listening to the doctors telling me what we needed to do next. I'd transfer to the delivery area because we needed to get this baby out. I had to decide if I was pushing this baby out or getting a cesarean section. I needed to prepare for the birth of a child I'd never get to take home. I needed support.

I called Mami.

They moved John Anthony and me to the delivery suite. My blood pressure was too high to move forward, so they started IV meds to help bring it down. The nurses brought toys and games for John Anthony and played with him. With his mami calm, he returned to the business of being five. Mami, Papi, and my brothers showed up at the hospital. My brothers whisked my boy away to give him attention, and Mami sat with me in my grief. I couldn't touch my belly. I wanted to get this over with as soon as possible. The doctor came into the room, checked my blood pressure, and decided it was time.

"Ok, Ms. Martinez, it's time to decide. Are we inducing labor or doing a c-section?"

Fresh tears burned my eyes, "I can't push this baby out."

The doctor nodded, "Let's get you prepped for surgery, then."

The details of the next few hours are spotty in my memory. It's interesting the things trauma imprints in your brain. I remember the smell of burning flesh as they cauterized the layers of flesh they cut to get Jean Carlos out of my womb. I remember Mami by my side. I remember sitting in a separate area of the hospital—a unit reserved for mothers who've lost the babies they prayed for. Sitting there, I didn't have to hear the wails of healthy infants or the cries of joy as new life entered the world. It was quiet in a way that was almost eerie and made me yearn to be home.

When they brought Jean Carlos in to see me, he was wrapped in a hospital blanket like any newborn—a tiny hat sat on his head. His mouth was a perfectly shaped bow, and his eyes closed as if sleeping the exhausted slumber of a newborn baby. He was perfectly formed, beautiful, and gone. If he'd been born three days prior, he'd have been a healthy baby boy. The hospital took pictures of Jean Carlos and me. In the days I spent recovering, family and friends visited, but I was in a fog and didn't even remember who was there. For weeks afterward, Mami would mention someone's visit, and I'd have no memory of it.

I couldn't wait to leave the hospital area coated in desperation and lost dreams, but returning to the home John Anthony and I set up to welcome his baby brother home wasn't easier. The house was full of baby supplies. As an excited, expectant mother, I had visited my favorite stores regularly and bought baby outfits in every size we'd need in the first months when a child grows in leaps and bounds. But Jean Carlos wouldn't grow. He wouldn't wear these clothes, and he wouldn't sleep in the bassinet. I couldn't stand being around these items. I immediately began donating, returning, and disposing of items. My brother and his wife were expecting and took much of the baby equipment. Most stores wouldn't take back merchandise with receipts and tags because it had been too long since I purchased them.

One day, I gathered up all the items I purchased from Marshalls and wandered in, dumping the items on the counter. The clerk remembered me visiting the store each week as my belly and excitement grew. She gasped when she saw me returning baby clothes with tears in my eyes.

"Oh my goodness. I'm so sorry," she said, hurrying to get the manager.

Though most of the items were past their return date, the clerk convinced the manager to refund me and take the clothes, toys, and blankets off my hands. Eventually, I managed to get rid of every trace of the baby I lost except a small box containing the photos from the hospital, Jean Carlos's death certificate, a blanket John Anthony decided to keep, and a card with tiny footprints.

Somehow, in the darkest times of your life, you're expected to make sound decisions about the funeral and burial of your precious child. I was supposed to be awake all night nursing, not arguing with my mother about the merits of cremation versus a Christian burial. Lacking the fortitude to plead my case, I acquiesced to my mother's wishes and agreed to a burial for Jean Carlos with the caveat that I would be able to see his precious face one more time before the service.

The day of the funeral dawned cold and unforgiving. The wind chilled us despite the layers we wore. The burial was set for a few days later, but a snowstorm pushed it off again and again. When the weather cleared enough to lower the casket into the ground, the funeral home wouldn't allow me to see Jean Carlos as we agreed.

"You don't want to remember him this way. It's been too long," the undertaker cautioned.

Still numb, I stood by the grave with family and a few friends on January 6, 2013. We wrapped Jean Carlos's casket in a photo blanket with pictures of John Anthony and me smiling and living a life we wanted to bring Jean Carlos into. Before they lowered the casket to the ground, my boy let go of my hand, draped his small body over the box holding his baby brother, and wept. It took a few of us to pull him away so they could commit my baby's body to the earth. In the days after seeing his tiny casket lowered into the frozen ground I felt terrible about leaving Jean Carlos in the cold. I was his mother, I was supposed to protect him and I just left him there.

Over the coming weeks, I'd slowly climb out of my grief for brief periods, mostly because I had to be a mother to John Anthony. He deserved that and more. I'd go through the motions of preparing meals, bathing him, reading him stories, and holding him close, but then I'd retreat to my bedroom and sit with John Carlos's box open. I'd scan through each photo, trace the outline of his tiny footprints, and try to catch a whiff of baby smell from the blanket. During this time, I realized I hadn't seen my best friend, who I'll call Maria, at the hospital or funeral.

During a phone call a few weeks after the burial, I asked, "Maria, did you come to the funeral? I don't remember seeing you." I imagined I'd probably missed her in my fog of grief.

She inhaled audibly, "I'm sorry. Whatever energy you have around you that caused you to lose your child, I can't be around. I'm pregnant, and I can't risk having that energy in my life. I came to the funeral, but I stayed in my car. I cannot be around you."

I can offer a woman like that empathy and understanding, but if someone's limiting beliefs and small-mindedness keep them from adequately showing up when they're needed by loved ones, I cannot allow them a seat in my circle. Losing Maria hurt because I considered her a sister. I was the godmother to her children. She showed her true self and capacity for love and acceptance, and I decided that if I kept friends like her, I wouldn't need enemies. Not every woman in your tribe will move with you to the next level. Sometimes people you're close with will show you they can no longer be part of your support system.

Once John Anthony returned to school, I found myself spending days alone, sitting in my dirty chair of grief and crying. After some time, I realized I was spending too much time sitting in a dirty chair. I was missing out on the joy of my child asleep in the next room. Jean Carlos's death pulled me completely away from my purpose. People around me told me that Jean Carlos's death was God's will, and I simply needed to find a way to accept that. These people believe that the death of a baby or any grand loss is God's way of punishing us or showing us we aren't yet worthy of his grace. But that doesn't fit my view of God, nor is it helpful when you're sitting in a grief chair and needing a way out. I needed a different kind of support. I found a grief therapist who would see John Anthony and me. I needed guidance to help get out of the dirty chair and reconnect with myself and my purpose.

When I work with clients moving through grief, I tell them grief is like the ocean. Waves flow in and out at different rates depending on the tides and how the weather affects the water. Small waves of grief include sadness or a fleeting memory. Sometimes small waves come as a subtle feeling of discontent when you wake in the morning. You learn to see these moments without feeding them. You acknowledge you're feeling off but don't allow the storm to overwhelm you. Through therapy, I learned not to let these small waves knock me off balance.

The larger waves roar in like a hurricane. Anxiety and depression weigh so heavily that you can't pull yourself out of bed, followed by a crash of anger and disbelief. You thrash against the shore, and the waves cascade over your head, filling your mouth like a scream. You find yourself negotiating with God, and it feels like you'll never pull yourself out. The current of the grief ocean is too strong. Those are the moments you need tools to move through. Sometimes you need a life vest— some buoyancy while you navigate the waters yourself. Other times you need a raft or rescue boat full of people who can pull you along. When the water is so overwhelming that you cannot catch your breath—when the depression threatens to sink you— you may need a helicopter to pull you to safety and a full rescue team to hold you together. In those moments when the waves of grief threatened to overwhelm me I remembered that my God would never leave me to battle alone. As long as I was willing to put in the work He would do his part to ensure I found calmer seas.

Eventually, you learn to honor those waves. You ride your grief waves with the grace of a surfer instead of fighting them. You experience the emotions but pull yourself back to the center. When you can do this, you focus on your path again. When you're reconnected with your purpose, it's like the ocean on a peaceful morning. Smooth as glass, but with the powerful potential flowing underneath. In those moments, you can learn to use the undercurrent of your grief to fuel your purpose.

My purpose is to raise a strong man. John Anthony and I learned together to manage the grief process. We journaled about Jean Carlos and about how we missed his presence. I wrote in my room or any time grief felt overwhelming. John

Anthony had a small notebook he'd carry to school daily and fill with notes and pictures about his feelings whenever he felt the need. I did the same. I used my grief to model how we behave when life seems too much for my son. In the moments I felt most desperate, I talked with God. One day, sitting on my bed, Jean Carlos's box spread out around me. I told God I wouldn't ask him why he took my baby. There's never really a reason for such things. He didn't want to punish or teach me a lesson—my God is not vindictive. Instead, I asked him to lead me to a way to use my grief to further my purpose on this earth.

My purpose is to help others heal. This came to me, as it always does when I spend time getting quiet and paying attention to what's true for me. The best way to heal myself is to use my skills to heal others. In helping others find themselves, find strong relationships, and process grief and trauma I'd be able to better handle my own. I recommitted myself to my work in therapy practice. For a while, that felt like enough. I reconnected with myself, helping others, and my son grew strong enough that, by the end of the summer, he decided he didn't need grief therapy any longer. We were thriving, at least most of the time.

In the years after losing my baby, my grief lost its intensity, and I turned toward John Carlos's memory box less and less. As I write this book, it sits in my bedroom drawer. I haven't opened it in about seven years. I no longer need tangible items to remember my lost son. I have memories, purpose, and a beautiful family. But, somehow, I felt there was more to my purpose—that I was meant to channel my grief in a different way. In 2019 I finally knew how.

It wasn't until 2019 that I understood exactly the impact I could have. It happened like most of the moments that bring clarity to your dreams—a small moment you could miss if you aren't looking for it. I had a friend I hadn't heard from in some time. I reached out via text message on a random weekday while seeing clients.

I've been thinking about you.

When she responded, we made plans to meet for coffee.

Sitting across from her, a latte steaming in front of me, my friend said, "You don't understand how huge your presence is in my life. When you sent me that message, you interrupted a suicide attempt. I read your message and remembered that someone in this world cared and that my life mattered. You saved my life."

She went on to tell me about the abuse she suffered as a child at the hands of her father. My resolve to help others heal and create a life they love solidified that day, and I began looking for another opportunity to use my adversity as a path to healing others.

I turned Jean Carlos's memory into a foundation dedicated to helping single mothers of students with special needs in the Dominican Republic thrive. Since its inception, JC's Precious Minds Foundation has helped mothers find resources for their special needs children. We provide help with housing, psychological testing, therapies (occupational, physical, and speech), psychiatric services, clothing, private education, and specialized food for those with sensory issues. In 2022 the foundation received 501c3 status qualifying us as a nonprofit and increasing our ability to raise funds and provide tax-free assistance to more families.

With each child the foundation helps, I'm reminded of the gift of Jean Carlos's brief time in my world. I embrace the memories of him dancing salsa in my belly and kicking my ribs when I tried to sleep. I am grateful for the evenings spent curled up with John Anthony reading to the baby brother in my belly, and the way those experiences shaped my boy, who is now a thriving young man. I'm grateful for the opportunity to use my skills and adversity to help other women heal from grief and trauma, reconnect with their purpose, and channel their adversity into triumph.

Grief is part of being human. When we hope and work diligently, we often mourn the loss of a dream instead of celebrating achievement. When we love, we get to ride the highs of that connection, but also understand that we will grieve its loss at some point in our lives. Grief can take many forms, lasting weeks, months, or years. Sometimes it's always there lending a sharp edge to your life experiences moving forward. For me, there are days I wake up and feel particularly exhausted and out of touch. My body craves rest, and my mind struggles to focus on the day's tasks. On those days, I am grieving. I honor it and offer myself the care and attention I'd give a best friend or child dealing with difficult emotions because I know I will bounce back.

But grief is not a bad thing. Grief is a sign of your human capacity to love, to hope, to work, and to dream. Grief is energy. When you're grieving, you have a choice. You can allow it to swallow you and steal your power, or you can decide to get out of the dirty chair and find a way to channel the energy of your grief into something that builds the legacy you want to create. I'm not telling you to get over it right away—grief doesn't work that way—but I am saying that you get to decide at some point. You get to open your toolbox, find support, reach out to connect with others, journal, and reconnect with your purpose. Developing a toolbox to manage grief is essential if you're creating a legacy because any life worth living comes with loss. If you're embracing love, dreams, and challenges, another experience with grief is likely right around the corner. I know it was for me.

Chapter Takeaways

❖ Adversity and crisis weren't meant to take you out.

❖ Never ask yourself why you experience adversity. Instead, ask what the purpose is.

❖ Grief is like the ocean; it has big waves, small waves, and periods of calm.

❖ When you find yourself in the dirty chair of grief, honor it.

❖ Grief is a personal experience, but we can still teach our children to honor and move through it.

❖ In times of adversity, we must always reach out to our support system.

Self-Evaluation Prompts

❖ What are you grieving? This may be the loss of a person, pet, career, or relationship.

❖ Identify the feelings, thoughts, and behaviors impacting your life and/or business.

❖ How do you want to honor your grief or loss?

❖ What tools and strategies can you put in your grief toolbox to help you honor and move through the experience? This could be therapy, meditation, coaching, self-care practices, reaching out to friends, etc.

❖ How do you want to feel about your loss? How do you want to behave? How do you want to interact with the world in a more positive way?

Part 3

Choosing Me:
Why Selfish is Better
Than Selfless

*To build a dream life you must stop living
according to family or societal pressure.
It comes down to trust in the
co-creation process.*

Chapter 6

Surviving Brain Surgery

Adversity didn't destroy your GIFT;
it came to prove your gift!
Adversity and crisis weren't meant to destroy you,
they were meant to build you.

The air conditioning chased away the July humidity as I opened the door of Lucinda's beauty salon. Tears stung my eyes—they'd been my perpetual companion these days. Despair followed me everywhere. I felt grateful Lucinda scheduled me when others weren't in the salon. I could let her see my sadness, but I didn't want to share it with the world. She called my appointments "us time." It was always a special time. I flopped into her chair and exhaled. That's how it always felt to sit in her salon. Lucinda had been my stylist for years, and she became more of a friend than a service provider. I'd always been adventurous with my hair, often changing from short hair to long, playing with color and texture, and allowing my trusted stylist to play in their art form. This visit, though, would prove to be much more than art. Lucinda proved herself to be one of the most powerful women in my support system.

I sat in the chair, peering at our reflection in the mirror as Lucinda stood behind me. Her hands whispered lightly over my shoulders, letting me know I was safe and cared for at that moment. I began to spill my troubles the way women do in a stylist's chair.

"Tell me, Mamita, what's going on with you today?" Lucinda's lyrical voice questioned.

"I just feel so lost. I can't plan anything because I don't know what will happen after this surgery. Most people don't even make it out of this alive, and those that do—," my voice broke.

Lucinda let a small smile curve her lips, and her hands continued caressing my shoulders, encouraging me to continue.

"I just finished filling in my will and creating a trust for John Anthony, and I just feel hopeless. Like everything is being taken away from me, and I don't have any say over it." I let the tears fall. "I've always been the woman in control, working my plan, creating my life. And now, I just have to go along with all this nonsense. I don't even get a say in how this goes!"

I glanced up, tears blurring my vision, and saw Lucinda's eyes mirroring my sadness. She never tried to tell me it would all be okay. She didn't patronize me with empty words. She bore witness to my pain the way Queens learn to do for one another. She sat with me in my dark place and held space for me to purge the negativity from my body.

I just can't imagine leaving my boy without a Mami. I'm his whole world," I continued, "We already had to stop breastfeeding because of my treatments, and I just don't know how much more I can ask him to take at just three years old."

"And when is your surgery?" Lucinda never told me to calm down.

"It's in September. I don't even know why I'm here getting styled. They're just going to shave my hair off at the hospital anyway. I can't even control my hair."

Lucinda tilted her head, letting her fingers play across my scalp, "What if we take back some control today?"

I raised an eyebrow, "What did you have in mind?"

"Well," Lucinda paused, circling around the chair, "You feel like you don't have control of anything in your life right now. That's a terrible feeling to carry around. We could just cut your hair here instead of waiting for the doctor to do it. We can shave it short. Give you something sexy and sassy rather than letting some butcher with a straight razor play barber when you're all vulnerable in a hospital gown." She found her way behind me again. She leaned over my shoulder, her eyes locking on mine in the mirror, "So, what do you say? You want to get back some control? You want to walk out of here looking super hot?"

I couldn't hold back my smile, "Now, you're talking my language. Let's do it. I'm ready. I was born ready." Those are always my favorite words when I feel I have regained my power.

With that, Lucinda and I made magic happen in that salon. She joined me in my struggle, heard me, and helped pull me out of my dirty chair. I walked in feeling desperate, sad, disempowered, and alone. I walked out, reminded that I was a force of nature capable of finding her power in any storm. When you have the right women in your tribe, they'll remind you again and again why you chose them.

I walked out of there with the sides of my head shaved short and extensions with a few blond streaks thrown in for extra attitude. I felt powerful, I felt in control, and I felt sexy as hell. A few weeks later, dressed for my best friend's birthday party in New York City, I posed for a photo wearing a fuchsia cocktail dress, gold heels, and a sultry look. I looked like the Dominican American Goddess I am. I knew I could make it through this experience by embracing the parts I could control and surrendering to those I couldn't.

Before we talk about how I learned to surrender, though, we must travel back to the fall of 2009 when a phone call changed my life—and threatened to end it. When I parked my car, my mind was racing through the list of last-minute items I needed to purchase before John Anthony and I traveled to Panama for vacation. It was November, and the chill in the air spoke of the impending snow. My phone rang, interrupting my packing list. "Hello?" I answered it somewhat exasperated.

"Hi, is Ms. Martinez available?" a deep male voice asked.

"May I ask who's calling?"

"It's Doctor Sythe."

"This is she," I glanced at my watch, conscious of the time.

"I'm calling with the results of your MRI. Unfortunately, your MRI shows that you don't have just one but two aneurysms. We need to sit down and discuss the next steps."

I dropped my pocketbook back onto the passenger seat. I listened as the doctor detailed the risks of living with an aneurysm, the surgery I'd need, and how difficult recovery would be. As he talked about surgical risks, I watched dried leaves float into the air and land on the hood of my SUV. A roaring in my ears drowned out the doctor's voice. I was in shock. I was confused and frozen.

Eventually, the call ended, and I hung up. I looked down at my phone still in my hand and knew I needed to reach out for support. I called Mami, then Papi, and then my Aunt Celia. Celia had a brain aneurysm burst during her last trimester with her youngest child and needed surgery. I knew she'd understand my fear. I relayed information, but none of the doctor's recommendations were sinking in. I didn't know what to do next, but I knew I'd need my people around me to get through it. I was supposed to go to Panama with my little boy and our friends. One moment I was planning life, building a dream, and making things happen. I was a woman rooted in her own power. It only took a moment for that to disappear and leave me frozen in place with life happening to me.

I knew that, at any moment, one or both aneurysms could rupture, and I'd be gone from my little boy's life. I forgot about the trip to Panama and drove to pick John Anthony up from school. The next few weeks passed, but I don't have many memories of them. I was floating through life—bathing my son, feeding him meals, reading him stories—but I wasn't really present. I went through the motions at work too. I saw my clients and listened to their problems, offering what support I could, but I couldn't focus. I was frozen in time. Looking back, I know I was stuck in the denial stage of grief. Instead of fighting to live, I was grieving the opportunity to see John Anthony grow into a handsome, intelligent, and successful man before it was even gone.

Living in that stuck place, I didn't even know what the first step was to move forward. How do you begin a medical process that could kill you? I ignored calls from my doctor and did not schedule follow-up appointments. It's not that I didn't want to take care of myself—I just didn't know how to unfreeze myself. I decided to sit in that dirty chair of grief instead of fighting. Then, I received a letter from my doctor's office.

Ms. Martinez, it is imperative that you give us a call and schedule a follow-up appointment with Dr. Scythe to discuss your treatment options. This is a very serious health matter, and you must give us a call.

I couldn't shake the fog of grief. I couldn't bring myself to act. In my mind, I was dying. I started seeing a psychologist because I knew something needed to change.

After I explained how I couldn't seem to move forward, she said, "Soribel, if you think you are going to die, you are going to die. You need to transform your mindset, perception, and how you see this crisis in your life."

She called me out. I was sitting in a dirty chair for so long that I allowed the grime of defeat to seep into my pores. I needed to get up, I needed to fight, and I needed to live because I had too much left to do still on this earth. If I gave up, I was giving up on my family, my dreams, and my son.

Adversity is never meant to destroy us. Adversity exists to show us how to manage a shit-storm and redirect our energy to what really matters.

I needed to stop letting life happen to me and start making things happen because that's who I am. I was walking around with a vague desire of, "I don't want to die." A vague desire produces vague results. When we don't know what we want, we are handed whatever is left. I don't like leftovers. I am Soribel, Dominican-American, daughter, mother, therapist, and Queen. I do not accept the bare minimum, but that's what I'd been giving myself.

To get strong results, I needed to get clear on my desire. I needed to state what I wanted and then find a way to get it. After that conversation with my therapist, I decided I wanted surgery from the most qualified doctor I could find. I decided I wanted the best outcome possible. I didn't want to live in fear of a ruptured aneurysm. I had too much to do. I had a greater impact to make in this world and unfinished dreams of entrepreneurship and motherhood. I was on the road to becoming my own hero and needed to stop letting an aneurysm derail my plans.

So, I turned to my co-creator and prayed, "God, show me the path. I know you are working on my behalf. I know you are always doing your part. I am willing to do my part in this co-creative process." I knew I had to take action—inspired and massive action.

I would stop settling into the dirty chair and start living intentionally again. I thought about this co-creation process with God and shifted my mindset away from the worst-case scenario because those thoughts kept me stuck in my filthy chair. I declared what I wanted. I wanted to be around to raise John Anthony because I never entered motherhood to raise a boy—I wanted to raise a man. I wanted to heal so I could help others heal. So, I embraced hope and my capacity to do what I needed to do to fulfill my part of this bargain with my co-creator. Of course, I knew that the surgery could go badly, and I knew the aneurysm could burst before I even had a chance to make it to the operating table. But I needed to focus on what could happen if everything worked out. What if everything goes perfectly? What if God and I could co-create the outcome I wanted? How might that feel?

I journaled about what I wanted my life to be after surgery. I detailed how I wanted to feel. I wrote about how I wanted to think after surgery. In that journal, there was no room for negative outcomes. I wrote a plan for how I would come out of surgery whole and healthy. I shifted my mindset and perception of that medical journey with each entry I wrote. I had to believe anything good I could imagine was possible. I manifested not just survival but getting back to being a thriving empowered woman with a dream once again.

God was going to love me and see me through this nightmare, but he wasn't going to find a specialist willing to operate, give me a year off work, or find the support team I'd need to make it through. I realized my responsibility in the co-creative process was to activate my power and ensure I did my part. I visualized the result I wanted. I saw myself walking out of a successful surgery and embracing my beautiful boy.

When we're handed a storm of adversity, we don't need to settle for what's given to us. Whether we face challenges in business, health, relationships, or any other part of building a beautiful life, we don't need to settle. We are worthy of the best care and the best team of people to help you. The trick is to find the parts of the experience you can control and work those angles as much as possible.

Often, finding what you can control means educating yourself. When you're leaving a relationship, that may mean finding resources in the community to help. If you're building a business, you'll need to ensure you reach out to leaders in your field for guidance. When the shit-storm you're going through is medical, that means reading, researching, and getting to know your problem more intimately than anyone else. An educated woman is a powerful woman. A woman who can organize her knowledge and communicate it clearly has even more power. When you seek education, you can make better decisions and more readily identify the people you need as part of your journey. Educating yourself will help you decide what you need, what you want, and what tools you need to stay out of the dirty chair.

I embarked on a journey of education. I learned all I could about brain aneurysms, particularly my aneurysms. I learned that the neck of the aneurysm was too wide for a non-invasive procedure that would clip the neck and prevent it from bursting. I learned that I needed a surgeon who only worked on aneurysms. I needed a medical professional whose knowledge exceeded mine so I could be assured my brain—and my life—were in competent hands. My medical diagnosis was out of my control, but finding the right medical team was not.

I prayed again, "God, please put the people, resources, and support I need in my path to health."

Armed with the knowledge that I was not alone, I had the strength to move through the next step with my faith in God. I embarked on a mission to find what and who I needed. I traveled with Mami for consultations with neurosurgeons in Florida, Cleveland, New York, and Boston. Some of these consultations were completed via telemedicine. I met with every local doctor in Danbury, New Haven, and Hartford. I'd walk into each consultation with a pile of medical paperwork, images of my brain, and a growing pile of knowledge about my situation and the likely outcomes.

I heard that my case was too complicated and that surgery didn't carry a good enough chance of survival. I heard that doctors refused to operate and advised that I get my affairs in order and wait for one of the aneurysms to burst. That plan didn't fit the one my co-creator and I made. I was fighting—I was doing my part, and He was doing His.

By the time I walked into Dr. Carucci's office, I knew exactly what type of brain aneurysm I had and the outcome I wanted. He sat across from me in his office, and I slid the giant folder containing all the bad news I'd gotten over the past months.

"Well, Ms. Martinez, it seems you're a woman who knows what you want. How can I help you?"

"I want surgery to fix the aneurysms."

"This is a complicated case."

"If you or your family came to me as a therapist, would you want to solve the problem yourself? Do you want me to solve your problem? How would you feel if I told you your trauma was too complicated and sent you on your way to suffer without hope?"

"Fair point. I'll need two weeks to review your files. I can tell you know exactly what you're looking for, and I want to find a way to give it to you."

Two weeks later, sitting across from Dr. Carucci at a conference table in his office, I nervously anticipated his recommendations. In that meeting, he did what no other doctor had been able to do. Dr. Carucci took out a piece of paper and a pencil. Without opening my file, he diagramed my aneurysms down to every detail. He explained their structure and why he would choose to do a microsurgical clipping with a craniotomy instead of the less-invasive endovascular coiling other doctors wanted to try. He told me what I already knew—that coiling wouldn't work for my aneurysm because the neck was too wide, and the coil could slip out, causing a stroke.

During the surgery, they'd have to shave my head and break open my skull from my forehead to my ear. A computer attached to micro cameras would project my brain onto a monitor during the surgery to assist the doctor in finding the aneurysms. Despite the frightening details of the surgery, Dr. Carucci's knowledge and willingness to explain everything to me gave me peace, filled me with trust, and reassured me that he knew what he was doing. He only repaired brain aneurysms and was local, so my family and I wouldn't have to travel long distances for treatment. Dr. Carucci's competence removed many barriers and financial stress about the surgery.

Even after shifting my perception of my medical nightmare, reworking my mindset, educating myself, and finding the right support, there were still plenty of days I sat in the dirty chair of sadness, overwhelm, and grief. I knew the chances of a successful surgery were slim. I knew I could be paralyzed, become a vegetable, lose my ability to speak or lose my life. All I could do was honor my grief when it came up. I looked at the feelings, identified the thought that caused them, and then released it. I pulled myself out of the chair and did what I needed to do as a responsible co-creator. I reminded myself of what I truly desired—an opportunity to build my Queendom and the time to mother my boy.

I prayed to God to show me the path forward and recommitted to doing my part. This prayer has become my go-to prayer. It works for me. When I ask God to show me the path, He always does. I set up a living will and made decisions about what would happen if I could not function independently after surgery. I created a trust for John Anthony and wrote my will. I decided who would raise my boy if I was unable to.

When you're going through adversity, you will inevitably sit back down in the dirty chair. You will have hours and days where the negativity overwhelms you. All you can do is acknowledge the negative emotions, figure out what's causing them, and use your tools to pull yourself out of the chair. Be prepared to repeat this process regularly—if you're living life to your potential, you will occasionally crash.

I walked into the hospital in September with Mami and Papi beside me. John Anthony was with my mother's sister and would stay there until my staples came out, and I'd had an opportunity to recover. Dr. Carucci walked into the room after the nurses prepped me, wearing a suit, and looked like the capable doctor I trusted him to be. He handed me a pile of paperwork detailing the surgery's possible outcomes. He listed paralysis, speech problems, loss of motor control, and death. At some point, I stopped him.

"I know the risks. The list you're giving me will do nothing but put me back in a negative mindset. The only story I want to tell today is the one where the surgery is successful, and I walk out of here in a few days without death chasing me around."

Dr. Carucci nodded, handed me the forms to sign, and looked me in the eyes, "I'll see you soon. You are in good hands."

"I know I am. That's why I chose you," I replied.

An hour later, I saw Dr. Carucci one more time in the operating room. My nurses were there preparing everything for the procedure. The anesthesiologist sat waiting for the doctor's signal.

"Is there anything else you want to say or ask?"

"After surgery, if I ask you for a glass of orange juice, you'll know everything went okay, and my brain is working," I smiled at him.

"Alright, I'll see you in a little bit," Dr. Carucci said and signaled to the anesthesiologist.

When they woke me up, I was in a different room.

"Ms. Martinez?" A nurse stood over me.

I lay there, not responding, and did a mental status check on myself. I asked myself what year it was, who was president, where I was, and why I was in the hospital. When I felt satisfied that I wasn't a vegetable, I responded, "I want a glass of orange juice."

The nurse smiled and ordered my beverage.

"Hey, did everything go okay in there? Did you have to tie me down there? I remember feeling something on my leg," I said.

"I think everything went fine. Let me go ask the doctor." She hustled away like a surgical nurse with too many patients.

When Dr. Carucci returned to check on me. He assured me everything went as planned during the procedure.

"In the surgery, someone held my right leg down, and it hurt. I asked them to let me go because it hurt. The person holding my ankle said no, it's not your time. I can't let you go."

The nurse pulled up the bedsheet to check my leg. There were finger marks on my ankle. But no one held it down. At some point during that surgery, the stress and pain became too much, and I wanted to let go. But it wasn't my time. I believe my co-creator sent an angel to remind me that my work on this earth wasn't done—that I still had a purpose to fulfill.

The nurse looked up at me, "You are really a miracle. That was a really difficult surgery."

For the next several hours, I never felt the pain from my surgery and the wound on my scalp. The pain I felt radiated from the bruising on my ankle. When they transferred me to a regular room after recovery, my family stood around me, but all I wanted was my boy. I called John Anthony so he knew his Mami was okay.

Three days later, I walked out of the hospital on my own two feet, able to think, talk, and move as I wished. Tia Irene came from Spain to take care of me. She planned to stay until I recovered enough to care for my boy on my own. When I got home, however, all I wanted was my boy with me.

I called him, "I want to come home. I want you now, Mami," his little voice begged.

I turned to Tia Irene and asked to have my boy return to his home. My family decided they'd help me get what John Anthony and I both wanted and brought him to me.

He wandered into the bedroom and climbed next to me. "Mami, you look like a monster. Are you a monster?" John Anthony pointed at the staples on my scalp.

Hearing this was devastating. A three-year-old shouldn't have to go through seeing his mami like that. Suddenly I felt shame and guilt about not being the mother my son needed. It was another moment where despair threatened to overtake me. I needed to speak to myself more compassionately. I needed to remind myself that I'm a brave woman who could bounce back from this. The guilt and shame were not emotions I was going to feed.

"No baby, Mami had a procedure done. That's why I have these staples."

Despite my appearance and the limitation in my ability for a while, John Anthony was happy to be home. I felt grateful he could express his feelings openly and that I was there to guide him. Once able to drive, I resumed most of my mom duties as quickly as possible. I'd take my boy to school, then return home and take medication. I'd sleep so my brain could rest and heal. My alarm sounded shortly after 2:00 PM, and I'd go pick him up. John Anthony's preschool was incredibly supportive and sent meals home with us. With that and the support of my family, I had everything I needed to heal from surgery. Lucinda even ensured I had a custom-made sassy wig to wear when I wanted to cover my surgery scars.

I drove to Hartford for my two-week follow-up and walked into the office.

"Where's your driver?" Dr. Carucci asked when I sat in his office.

"I drove myself."

"I can't believe how well you're doing. You are a miracle."

At that appointment, after removing the staples and checking to ensure I was healing well, Dr. Carucci invited me to be part of a team to help improve the hospital's services in the stroke department. Most of the people who have this surgery experience more complications. It's rare for patients to make it out as whole as I was, and the hospital wanted to improve its practice. I spent three years on that committee working to help them improve their services.

The committee met monthly to discuss the issues the stroke unit was dealing with. One of the problems in the unit was that it was too noisy for me while I stayed in the hospital after surgery. I could not rest, which is vital to let your brain heal. We made transitioning from surgery to other areas of the stroke unit smooth and pleasant for the patients. We also changed the registration and onboarding process to make it easier for families. Many patients came from the emergency room and would have to stay in the intensive care unit. We established emotional support for families and patients. After leaving the unit, the committee discussed support and resources that patients would need after discharge and provided aftercare calls and follow-ups to ensure patients and families adjusted well after surgery.

After a month, the days at home when John Anthony went to school made me crazy. My brain was ready to help others and be productive. In February 2011, I added a master's degree program to my workload. After putting John Anthony to sleep each night, I'd complete classwork, often staying up until the wee hours of the morning. I'd work during the day and repeat the long evenings because I wanted to achieve a goal. As always, my family supported me and cared for John Anthony to help make the dream of a master's degree a reality. I was busy and probably overextended, but I was incredibly grateful. I healed completely from my brain surgery because I had the support, the tools, and the understanding of how mindset can influence the outcome of the most difficult situation.

All women are worthy of love and care when dealing with adversity. The greatest love a woman can experience is self-love. When you love yourself fully and think yourself worthy of love, care, and guidance, you are more likely to join forces with the Universe to bring the healing you deserve. If you don't love yourself enough to care for yourself, find support, and nourish yourself, you cannot heal. You must love yourself enough to do the mindset work to get yourself out of a dirty chair as often as you need to. Deciding to move through adversity is the greatest act of self-love. Loving yourself is not selfish. It is selfish to love others and not extend the same level of love to you.

Chapter Takeaways

❖ Never let adversity be bigger than your purpose.

❖ Always choose life.

❖ Join God in the co-creative process, and do your part.

❖ Reconnect with your purpose and your creator when adversity knocks on your door.

❖ A Queen must have support to move through adversity and create the legacy she is meant to create.

❖ Love yourself enough to do the work.

Self-Evaluation Prompts

❖ Identify your adversity. What challenges are you facing right now?

❖ How is this adversity affecting your life, relationships, and business?

❖ What thoughts and feelings are you having about your challenges? Are they in alignment with your purpose?

❖ Identify your support system. Who can support you through your adversity?

❖ Visualize and describe the end result you want. How do you want to think, feel, and behave when your challenge is over?

❖ Identify a plan for overcoming this adversity, keeping the end result in mind.

Chapter 7

Healing Religious Trauma

God, show me the path. Help me heal and understand what the purpose of my creation is.

In 2020, in the middle of a global pandemic, I found myself sitting in a police station holding a letter that triggered deeply entrenched trauma. Police officers moved around me, conversations floating on the stale institutional air. I heard none of it.

Thirty years before, the church I attended had joined forces with a man to try to force me into a marriage I did not want. The letter I held in my hands in that police station was from him. I sat trembling, reliving the shame, fear, and self-doubt the church indoctrinated me with for over a decade. My phone chimed with message after message from him, telling me that God wanted us to be together and that he would do anything to ensure we would become man and wife. When the police called him and told him to stop, threatening arrest if he didn't, he became angry. That's when the threats started rolling in. His behavior triggered me, but he wasn't dealing with a naive 15-year-old girl this time. This time I was a grown-ass woman capable of taking care of herself, and I wasn't backing down.

As a young girl in the Dominican Republic, I enjoyed a life of family time, school, competitive volleyball, and hours playing with my neighborhood friends. When Papi moved to the United States and left my brothers and me with Mami, she needed connection and support. She found it in the Pentecostal Church. At nine years old, I was too young to understand how important this change would become in my life. My focus was on how the loss of things I loved compounded the grief of losing Papi. I remember no longer being able to wear pants or shorts. I found ways to play in my skirts, but the shorts ban meant I could no longer play volleyball. I was also forbidden to play with many friends I'd had my entire life. These people were now considered "of the world." I had no idea what that meant, but I was expected to obey the new rules.

Church services were hot and overstimulating. Even in the Dominican heat, women wore floor-length skirts and long sleeves and kept their heads covered. Songs rang out, their fervor eclipsed by testimonials of people certain the Holy Spirit had touched them in one way or another. The pastor preached about salvation and all the ways we could mess it up. The only reward for being pure and wearing suffocating clothing seemed to be getting into heaven, which I was completely uninterested in at the age of nine. I was more concerned with why I couldn't play volleyball, but no one seemed to have an answer to that, save for it being "against God's will."

There were other changes that had far-reaching consequences for my life, even if I didn't know it at the time—changes that led to shame I'd spend decades trying to unravel. As a child, you don't have much control over where you go and what you do anyway. So, though the late church services every night meant I was exhausted at school the next day, I went without question because Mami said I must. My education was always a priority before Papi left. Once we joined the church, education became secondary to religion. In fact, the church spoke out against education, telling the congregation that if we sought higher education and financial success, we'd go to hell. Education was now an afterthought. In addition to the late-night services, I now spent Saturdays and Sundays preaching on the streets and visiting people's houses to spread the "word of the Holy Spirit."

That first year without Papi, grades and academic performance suffered. I was reeling from the loss of Papi as a constant presence in my life and couldn't understand the other changes. Plus, I was just plain tired from the late nights and early mornings. Eventually, Mami moved to the United States, and religion lost its hold on my life for a brief while.

By the time my brothers and I joined Mami and Papi in the United States, she'd become a member of a new Pentecostal Church. It was a bit more lenient—especially in the rules for women and the frequency of sermons, but the basic teachings were the same. We had late-night services three times a week, plus Sundays. Papi originally joined us for Sunday services, but the church preached against education—saying that seeking education and financial success was against God's will. Papi was an

90

educated man who prioritized his children's education. For him, financial success was the path toward the future he wanted for my brothers and me. Eventually, he stopped going, but Mami demanded that my brothers and I attend services with her.

When the pastor's son died in gang-related violence, that church closed, and Mami quickly found another. My time at this new church was filled with shame, degradation, and terror. I was traumatized and scared when I left, yet still entrenched in the church's teachings.

As I grew into a young woman in our new church, I learned that women were responsible for controlling the sexual urges of men. We were not allowed to cut our hair—to cut the ends of it was cause for disciplinary action from the church elders. Modesty was required. Our skirts had to be long—often measured as we entered on Sundays. The pastor regularly sent me home because he said my skirts were too short. Once, I wore a skirt that met the length requirements but had a slit on one side. The pastor's wife pinned it before I was allowed to enter the church. I learned that wearing makeup, stockings, or perfume was a sin because it could cause a man to lust. I learned that by being a woman, I was to be hidden, quiet, and adhere to the teachings of my elders. My mother, yearning for community and a God who would fix the problems in her life if she was "good" enough, allowed these teachings to mold me and grow roots in my heart.

When I was 15 years old, the pastor and a few church elders began speaking of a prophecy of my husband. It was common for the congregation to pray for guidance about who young women should marry—it was a conversation I'd heard many times as one teenage girl after another came of age. I never expected they'd decide for me before I could even drive a car. There was a man in the church, I'll call Alicea, who converted to the Pentecostal Church and was saved. They told me it was God's will that I marry this person. Mami didn't agree with the decision of the church elders, but her fear of speaking against God's will kept her quiet.

The pressure to marry this person created cognitive dissonance for me. I was pulled in two different directions and learned that both were right—but the path of God did not allow for my dreams. At home, Papi spoke of college and career, encouraging my entrepreneurship dreams. Papi expected his children to go to college and graduate school. He didn't believe in the church's teachings about education and instead taught me about being an independent woman, knowing what I wanted, and going after it. With his guidance, I never gave up on my dreams. I continued my studies and dreamed of making enough money to afford a few luxuries and all the travel I wanted. Then, I went back to church and learned all those dreams that my father encouraged would send me to hell.

If I go to college, I'm going to hell.

If I have money, I'm going to hell.

If I don't get married to this man, I'm ignoring God's will, and I'm going to hell.

I didn't know how to conform to the church's teachings while staying true to what I knew to be my path. I continued working with the church, volunteering to participate in television and three radio programs teaching children about salvation and changing their lives by coming into Christ. In my private life, I still struggled with acculturating in the United States. I spent any time I wasn't at school or church in my room—the cognitive dissonance worsened my depression. I wasn't allowed to enjoy the normal milestones of my teen years, including proms, end-of-year celebrations, and getting together with friends because of the strict religious rules. I was lonely, isolated, and unsure of everything.

I began to question God.

"Why would you want marriage for me? I want to attend school, be an entrepreneur, travel, and build a dream. Why would you want something for me that I don't want for myself?"

God never answered, but I kept questioning. Something Papi often said to me carried me through this difficult time and helped me remember my power.

"Soribel, never do something that would bring you shame, never give in to the pressure of those around you, and do what is best for you and what is in alignment with your values."

Marrying Alicea was not in alignment with my desire. He was not the type of man that I would want to be the father of my children. At a church event, a woman of about 50 began pressuring me to attend a church event with Alicea. I lost it.

"No, I want nothing to do with him!" I yelled.

The woman grabbed me by the arm and beat me for my insubordination and refusal to accept God's will. I cried, both humiliated by her actions and ashamed that I wasn't willing to follow what people told me God wanted. The other church members around us stared but said nothing. A few moments later I found myself in the pastor's office with my assailant. The pastor reprimanded me for insubordination. The church never reprimanded the woman—they thought she was merely trying to impose God's will. No one called DCF. No one defended me, and I was too young to defend myself. But I wasn't too young to make up my own mind about how I would like to be treated. I knew something was happening to me that was not okay with my spirit, my heart, and my desires. I wanted to live in alignment with my values. Why couldn't I have God *and* an education?

I wanted to find a church that would keep me in good standing with God and ensure my entrance into heaven because I still very much believed that dancing to music or wearing short skirts would send me to hell. I found a church willing to accept me, but to become a member, I'd have to prove myself worthy as a woman.

The pastor who pressured me to marry Alicea and my maternal aunt told the new church pastor that I was already spoiled—that I'd had sex with Alicea. The new pastor sent me to get a virginity test from my pediatrician. My doctor was beside himself when I requested a vaginal exam to prove I hadn't had sex. But, since I was the patient, and didn't know better than to go along with my pastor's request, I demanded it. I needed to prove myself worthy, and the only way to do that as a young woman of the church was to prove I hadn't caused a man to lust after me or allowed anyone to violate me. As a grown woman looking back on these incidents, I know now that many adults failed me. I was a child—and any number of people should have called DCF or the police to intervene. My pediatrician, a knowing church member, or any of the other adults around me had the opportunity to intervene but chose not to.

I brought the report to the new church, and they allowed me entry. I stayed there through the rest of my teen years as a leader for the children's ministry. It wasn't until I was in college that the cognitive dissonance became too much for me to bear. All the sermons preached at services were against prosperity. They shamed those who sought economic growth and demanded frugality and acceptance of what we were given. Seeking education was evil—but I was in college and loving the experience. Finally, I had enough. I divorced from religion.

The pastor was angry and begged me to reconsider. He threatened that I'd go to hell.

"I'd rather go to hell educated and rich than go to heaven ignorant and stupid."

With that, I marched out of the church and into my life as a student. But I was still traumatized. The trauma just manifested differently. I did a complete one-eighty and decided that God and anything having to do with God was the problem. I lived angry and resentful. Because of the brainwashing I underwent growing up in the Pentecostal Church, I believed it was God and Jesus treating me poorly. I blamed God for my lack of sleep, my inability to dress as I wanted, and the physical abuse I suffered in the church. I still believed I was wrong to want more out of life. I still believed I was going to hell for my choices—I just decided I didn't care anymore.

One day, in college, I ran into Alicea, who told me that the pastor and church elders wanted him and me to marry to prove he'd been saved. He had a history of prostitution and had lived as a gay man, and the church wanted him to prove he was worthy. To do that, Alicea needed to have sex with a female, get married, and have children. That would prove that God changed him after he repented for his sins. The pastor and church elders thought I was the perfect candidate. But they weren't counting on the fact that I really knew what I wanted, and marriage was not part of my plan.

This conversation with Alicea helped me realize how spiritually broken I was. I hated not just religion but all religious people. I walked around with shame about my choices. All of that negative energy would only weigh me down. I needed to find a way to forgive myself and restore the parts of me that went missing when we joined the Pentecostal Church back when

I was nine years old. I needed to relearn what I knew about myself and God before the church took that knowledge away.

I sought therapy to help me heal. I used to think it was my fault because I allowed the church's teachings to grow roots in my brain and multiply. I blamed Mami for not protecting me. I blamed God. Through my work with my therapist, I learned that forgiveness is not about letting people off the hook for abominable behavior. Forgiveness, rather, is the process of stopping yourself from drinking poison, hoping other people are going to die. When you decide to forgive, you are saving your own life. It doesn't mean the person you forgive isn't responsible for harming you—they absolutely are. Rather, it is taking responsibility for your own healing. It's realizing that you are worthy because you are—not because you are a mother, wife, good Christian, or any other label the external world puts on you. You are worthy of love and care simply because you were created.

I forgave myself for accepting the church's teachings and for the ways I gave in. I acquired new healthy beliefs about spirituality and how to always stay connected to the source of my power. I had to forgive Mami and realize she was just as brainwashed as I. She was unable to help me because she couldn't yet help herself. I released my anger for the people who hurt me because I didn't want them taking up any more space in my life. I needed that space for my dreams.

The process of forgiveness for me was long and arduous—with backward steps and leaps forward. I worked with my therapist and also sought help through self-help books, training, and teachings. I read about spirituality, connecting with God, and my intuition. Eventually, I realized that I had all of the God I needed inside me. I learned to get quiet enough to hear His voice, and I created a prayer that I still use today when I feel lost or uncertain. One of the most important mindset shifts is knowing that I do not need interpreters when it comes to connecting and talking to my creator. I have direct access to Him. Nor do I need someone to tell me what is good for me. I have God's wisdom and intelligence to make decisions. He gave us all the power to decide because we can make good decisions.

"God, show me the path. Help me heal and understand what the purpose of my creation is."

When you find yourself stuck in the dirty chair of anger and resentment—that place where your gifts, your creativity, and your worth are stifled by negativity—you need to find forgiveness. Perhaps you need to forgive others. Often, we also need to forgive ourselves. No matter who you work on forgiving or what the offense is that requires forgiveness, the process is the same. In my work with clients, many find it very difficult to forgive, especially themselves. They were wrongly taught that forgiveness requires a reconciliation between them and the person who did them wrong, hurt them, or even violated them. Forgiveness is more like a release of the hold these negative experiences have on our emotional health. While you hold the energy of these heavy emotions in your soul, heart, and body, it destroys you deep inside and often manifests in your mental, emotional and spiritual health.

I often get asked, "Soribel, but how do I begin to forgive them or even myself?"

First, you must be willing to release and forgive. I was not ready to forgive until long after I left the church. That's often the case. It can be difficult to forgive when traumatic events are still very close. Eventually, when I felt ready I wrote in my journal, "God, help me release these feelings. Show me how to let it go." I had to pray for the strength to forgive because anger over these experiences was holding me back from the life I wanted. I wanted the sort of freedom that is only available when you forgive yourself and others.

Second, you have to love yourself enough and have enough compassion for yourself that you can forgive yourself for your part in whatever took place. I needed to develop the compassion to see my acceptance of the religious teachings as the brainwashing it was and release myself from guilt over it. I always tell my clients, "It's not your fault what they did to you, but it is your responsibility to heal yourself because you deserve freedom."

Then, you need to understand that forgiveness is a gift for you, not for others. You never even have to tell other people you forgive them. You don't have to see them or speak to them at all. When I forgave the church for how they treated me and the lies they indoctrinated me with, I never said a word to them.

I did not sing kumbaya or join them for a meal. Forgiveness is an internal process we use to heal ourselves.

Finally, when you're ready, you must release your anger toward the people who harmed you. Anger exists to tell us we need to act—we need to change something about our lives. My anger at the church showed that I needed to get out. Once I got enough distance, I didn't need that anger any longer. But, I held onto it. Anger is a difficult dirty chair to rise from. It feels comfortable and safe because it protects us from vulnerability. Releasing the people who wronged you honestly means you let them back into your life. It means you no longer allow them control over what you think about yourself, who you are, and what you can do with your one precious life.

Throughout the process, you'll need to rely on support from people who understand what forgiveness is and who will help you forgive yourself and release your anger. I was lucky to have an incredible therapist, Dr. Kaplan, and several other women around me who believed in me and my dreams. I learned through healing my religious trauma that I should never question my worth as a woman or as a human. I am worthy of all the greatness there is in the universe because God created me as part of that universe. Even if her path shifts and changes, a woman who walks with God can always reach her destination. For me, the destination has always been grace, love, support, and purpose.

The tricky thing about trauma is that even when we heal it never fully goes away. Thirty years after I divorced the church for good and went on my journey of spiritual healing and discovery, I found myself sitting in a police station begging for help. Somehow, he'd found me.

When the man showed up at my office, my receptionist told him I was unavailable because he didn't have an appointment. He sat and waited for two hours before asking for a piece of paper to write me a letter. By the time I arrived, he was gone. I strode in, confident in my suit—a woman living the dream she'd cultivated for decades. My receptionist handed the letter to me, and I walked into my office to read it.

Before I walked away, my receptionist stopped me, "That man showed up and waited for two hours. He was really scary. Is everything okay?"

God spoke to me. He told me that you are my life part-
ner. He told me he loved me and wanted you, Soribel,
to be in my life. Please call me.

Alicea

I immediately began shaking. I was transported back to
the church building, where I had to prove my virginity. I relived
the physical abuse from church elders. I had a full post-trau-
matic stress disorder response, including all the sadness, despair, shame, and self-hate the church preached. I could smell the
building and the perfume of the woman who attacked me.

I walked back to my receptionist's desk on shaking legs.
"Cancel all of my appointments."

I needed to care for myself the way no one cared for the
younger Soribel, who was abused and pressured by the church.
I went home and found Alicea on Facebook. I sent him a message.

Please do not contact me again. Do not call me. Do not
come to my office. Do not send me letters or emails. Do
not contact me at all. This is my only warning. After
this, I'm going to the police.

Three bubbles popped up, Alicea was responding.

But we cannot go against God's word. His prophecy is
that we are to be married.

I reached out to my brother, who contacted Alicea and
told him to stop harassing me. I called on my support team,
family, friends, and one close friend who worked as a detective.
She encouraged me to go to the police immediately.

That's how I found myself sitting in a police station
clutching a letter and fighting against the trauma response, trying to pull me under. The police called Alicea to issue that final
warning. Cease and desist, or he will be arrested.

But Alicea was driven by God. He sent me Facebook messages while he was on the phone with the officer. Only this time,

they were threatening. He was going to find me. He was capable of doing whatever it took to fulfill God's purpose.

The police issued a warrant for his arrest. We discovered that his history included theft, drug charges, and prostitution. For harassing me, Alicea received probation and a lifetime no-contact order. I am forever grateful that the police and investigators took me seriously. I wasted two weeks being unable to support my clients while dealing with this legal issue. I understood that I needed to protect myself. I was no longer that young woman who didn't know what to do or didn't have support from those who were supposed to protect her.

But, my work was not done. The experience with Alicea rekindled trauma, and I had to do the work to heal all over again. My fight-or-flight response kicked in, and my nervous system was on overdrive. I returned to therapy and reprocessed the grief, pain, and fear. I had to reestablish in my mind my beliefs about myself, my purpose, and my connection with my Creator. I had to remember who *my* God is. My God is love, direction, and trust. My God is never vindictive. My God doesn't punish me for dreaming. He pushes me to dream bigger. I am a spiritual woman.

When you've healed from the trauma, you must understand that it will likely be triggered at some point. You must learn what your triggers are. When activated, you must return to basics.

Go to therapy.

Move through your healing process.

Forgive yourself.

Go find healing by healing others.

Do the work: meditate, journal, affirmations.

Connect with people who reflect the true version of yourself back to you.

Give yourself the love and support you'd give your best friend.

You must find your version of a higher power. For me, this is God, and sometimes I call him my Creator. Some people believe in the universe, karma, Buddha, Allah, Angels, or an inner self. Whatever you want to call it is fine by me—but find it. Find it and use it to help pull you through the darkness and push you toward the beautiful life you're meant to create. We are not

just physical beings. We are spiritual, mental, and emotional beings, and living in alignment with our purpose is where we find
success.

Chapter Takeaways

- ❖ God is not in church.

- ❖ You don't need an interpreter between you and God. You have direct access to your creator.

- ❖ A woman who walks with God will always reach her destination.

- ❖ You are not at fault for what other people have done to you, but you are responsible for your own healing.

- ❖ Healing is not a one-stop shop. It's a lifelong journey.

Self-Evaluation Prompts

- ❖ Identify a situation that caused you trauma—religion, abuse, domestic violence, a traumatic accident.

- ❖ Identify those who can help you heal from trauma—therapist, friend, family.

- ❖ Identify ways you can immerse yourself in the healing process.

- ❖ Create a self-care plan that supports your healing—meditation, journaling, exercise, socializing, etc.

Chapter 8

The Broken Heart of a Woman

I have been hurt, I have been down, but I have also decided to heal, and rise up, unbroken.

As a little girl I was called Soribel, or Sori by most of my family, and Princesa by those closest to me. The first grandchild in Papi's family I was dolled up, dressed up, and my hair always perfectly polished. It didn't hurt that my rosebud lips and chocolate eyes caused passersby to comment on how adorable I was. I loved the attention as a young child, and I loved the gifts Papi's family showered me with. I had a play kitchen that really cooked food, all the newest dolls little girls around me wanted, and plenty of dress-up clothes so I could play princess whenever my heart desired. I learned to cook early, standing on a small stool next to Mami. By age eight I could cook many of the dishes she prepared without help. I followed Mami around the house, helping as she picked up after Papi, and then my brothers. I was a good student. I didn't realize at the time that all of those gifts, all the attention from Mami, and all of the focus on my appearance contained a larger message.

Mami, and the other women around me taught me through their actions as well as words that women were supposed to always put others first. We were caretakers. We were supporters of our husband's dreams. We were not dreamers. I was growing into a Dominican woman. I was a future Dominican wife, mother, and homemaker. I needed to learn to care for babies, cook Dominican specialties, and keep a home neat and organized. I should be pretty, well put together, quiet, and accept what was given me without question. There was only one problem. I was loud, and I was not all that interested in these traditional Dominican gender roles.

When family told me I would make a great mother when I grew up I'd correct them.

"I'm going to run a business," I'd say.

When they told me when I grew up I would be able to marry anyone I wanted because I was so pretty, I'd say, "I'm going to go to college instead. I want to write a book and travel to Paris."

My aunts would laugh and tell me I should be an attorney since I always seemed to have something to say that went against the norm. One aunt told me my dreams were bullshit—that I was dreaming too big. Who was I to think I deserved more out of life than the women around me? I should be grateful for a loving family, a husband who provides for me, and happy children just like the women who raised me. Women could have small businesses run out of their homes in their spare time, but they were never out in the world creating impact and building legacies.

"Watch me," I'd say, turning back to my play and retreating to the dreams inside my heart.

Thankfully, I had other influence as a young girl—the sort of influence that reinforces your wings when others try to clip your flight feathers. I had Papi. Each time Papi talked to me about my life and my dreams he broke down the gender roles the women in my life accepted as fact.

"You cannot rely on your beauty, Princesa," he'd tell me between sips of coffee in the mornings, "You need to have substance, develop your intellect, and be independent."

As a young girl I held onto those words with a fierce grip. I was pretty, but I was more than pretty. I was kind, but I was more than kind. I was a woman, but a woman was not limited by that label. As I grew older, Papi's messages kept the same flavor, but challenged more of the cultural beliefs handed to me by Mami, my aunts, and the Pentecostal Church. When the church told me a woman was only worthy of love and marriage if she refrained from sexual pleasure until marriage, Papi delivered a different message.

"Your worth is not in your vagina. Your value is not in your beauty. Your worth is internal. It comes from within you and once you understand that you will be an independent woman, " he told me during my teen years. "When you go on dates, have fun, be open to love, but take your own transportation, your own money, and make sure someone who loves you knows where you are. If a date decides not to pay for dinner, not to drive you home, or decides to get fresh, you need to be able to take care of yourself."

"What do you mean, tries to get fresh?" My church upbringing did not prepare me for the topics

"I'm a man too, Princesa. When a man pays for a drink or dinner, he has an intention. Sometimes. If he's a good man that intention is to get to know you better, and sometimes it's less sincere. Either way, don't depend on others. If you don't have the money to be out having dinner, then stay home and cook it yourself. Make your own money, and then seek a partner who matches you—or don't. Don't give up your power through vagina, feelings, or finances."

Throughout my childhood and young adult life whenever I had a decision to make, I knew I needed to do what was in alignment of my truth. I acted in ways that wouldn't leave me embarrassed or shamed. I had a cultural message, and I had Papi. Papi's mother, my abuela, was very independent. She raised five children alone when her husband emigrated to the United States. She started businesses, sought new learning, and never relied on a man to give her and her children what she needed or wanted. The lessons from Papi saved me and gave me a different perspective than the one I got from church. Papi's words helped reinforce who I was—the little girl who lay under the stars dreaming of business, books, and success. Every decision I make in life, in love, and in business, I make because I choose to, because I want to.

Papi was my hero. But, as with so many heroes, he had flaws. Children don't just learn what you teach them. They learn what they see and experience in their environment. Papi taught me lessons about independence and about knowing my value as a woman. But the way he behaved in his marriage to my mother did not reinforce those values. It's common in Latino culture for men to subscribe to machismo ideals, have extramarital affairs, and even father children with a mistress. As a child I developed a sense that all men were like my father—full of ideals they wish to pass on to their children, but behaving in ways that don't honor their values. Because that's what I thought of men, that's the sort of man I attracted. Hardworking providers lacking in emotional connection in relationship with their partners.

Until I started studying psychology I didn't understand why Papi could say one thing, but behave a different way. He saw women suffering in their marriages and he never wanted me to be stuck like them. He never wanted me dependent on a man. But, he continued to behave in ways that devastated my mother and broke her heart. I now know Papi did not do the internal work to shift his beliefs, behavior and emotions to align with his intellect. He grew up around men stepping out of marriages, his father even took him to visit his mistress when Papi was a child.

The women around me were unhappy in their relationships with unfaithful men. But, in conversation with each other they normalized the behavior.

"If he comes home to me, and I'm number one, what does it matter if he steps out?"

That statement, and many like it, didn't make sense to me. If you're number one, shouldn't your partner ensure your needs are met? I remember the times Mami found out about another woman Papi was seeing. Often, she'd cry and beg him to stop, occasionally she'd move out for a time. But, Mami always came back to Papi. She felt that it was important for us to have a father. I think she was scared to be alone raising three children and dealing with the judgement about being a single mother. Mami chose to continue dealing with Papi's cheating. So many women I knew did the same.

When women decided to stay in the relationships that caused them pain they were lauded for this choice. They were praised as strong women for allowing, taking disrespect, withstanding abuse, and taking care of their men. They were super moms, super wives. Women always stayed because the cultural expectations demanded they raise children and be married. Superwomen take care of everyone else and put themselves on the back burner. The superwomen I knew were codependent emotionally, spiritually, and financially.

I didn't want to be superwoman. I wanted to be a Queen. A woman who understands her worth, understands the support she needs, and isn't afraid to do the work to make it happen. My value didn't come from being a mom, a wife, a giver. My value came from being me—I was worthy because I was created.

Once I realized G was a man just like my father, I decided to be a single mother. That choice wasn't without worry, guilt, and fear of judgment. It was difficult as hell, but I wanted John Anthony to understand his mom had enough respect for herself that she would never allow a man to treat her like anything other than a Queen. I want my son to treat his future partner like the Queen she is. I wanted my words to be in alignment with my actions.

I speak with women all the time who chose their relationships for many reasons that have nothing to do with their desires, their needs, and their dreams. Women choose relationships because they don't want to break up with the father of their children. They choose relationships because society taught them they should be married by a certain age. Women accept less than they deserve in relationships to avoid judgment, or because of family pressure. Women choose relationships because they don't think they are capable of creating a beautiful, rich, full life without one. None of those reasons are reasons to invite another person into your life as fully as you need to in a partnership.

To empower yourself to only allow relationships in that support your dreams you first need to identify the unhealthy patterns and behaviors that lead you to choose relationships that don't align with your purpose. These relationships could be with family, your partner, friends, children, or even coworkers. There are patterns of thought and behavior that govern every relationship in our lives. For me, recognizing those patterns and the unhealthy relationships they caused meant cognitive behavioral therapy where I discovered how patterns I learned from my parents' marriage played out in my adult life.

Then, we need to recognize the distorted thinking that creates this problem. I thought all men were cheaters. I thought women couldn't expect more from the men they chose as partners. That distorted thinking didn't serve me. It led me away from my purpose and my vision. Once you find the distorted thinking that keeps you from creating relationships that support and encourage your dreams ask yourself if the thoughts are helpful. Find out where the thoughts come from, and then it's time to figure out what you get out of this distorted thought pattern.

When we let unhealthy patterns rule our lives it's typically because our subconscious mind gets something out of that thinking and behavior. Staying in an unhealthy relationship may cause other people to call you strong. If you surround yourself with people who aren't chasing their dreams it becomes easier to abandon your own. Is it fear of failure that's holding you back? Is it fear of success? Once we understand these motivations and behaviors we use problem-solving skills to deal with difficult situations about where they are in life right now.

If you want to shift, change, and transform patterns you can. Develop confidence in your ability to choose. I see especially in my female clients that they lack confidence in making the next right decision to move toward their goals. My confidence came from those conversations with Papi. He made me believe that no matter what, I was the shit, and I could make any decision I wanted.

In my work with coaching and therapy clients, we face fears instead of avoiding them. When you're afraid about making a decision in life, business, or relationships, you must face the fears and label them. This takes away the fear's power. Then, play in your mind how you want a situation to go—visualize the perfect ending. Realize you get to choose the end result.

I teach clients techniques to emotionally regulate themselves when they face a big decision. We use tapping, meditation, deep breathing, rest, exercise, and journaling to keep our bodies relaxed and our minds clear so we can hear divine guidance. We talk to people with similar values and while we can't avoid relationships with every naysayer in our lives—we can stop giving them a front-row seat to our dreams. We give our energy, attention, and focus to the relationships that fuel and inspire us.

Even now as an adult when I consult with Papi about a business strategy or a personal decision, he never tells me what to do. He told me as a child that my worth and my direction came from within. He listens—that's how he shows his love and support. But he never gives advice.

At the end of my first year in business, I surveyed clients about how they felt about our services and what other services they needed. I catalogued that feedback as part of an analysis of my entire business plan. My clients were clear about their needs.

They wanted group therapy, online courses, and medication management. I knew that would be a quantum leap for the business. The decision to offer online courses, medication management, and group sessions would drastically increase the number of people we could serve. It might create a larger impact on our community than I ever thought possible. That impact could lead to huge financial growth for the business, or it could be an giant mess.

I called Papi and told him about the client feedback.

"What do you think the next step is?" he asked.

I paused, inhaled and let my breath out slowly, "Well, I want to expand my services."

"You already have the answer, trust yourself and go do what you have to do."

The process of choosing relationships that serve you and eliminating those that don't is scary, heartbreaking work. Some of the people you've been closest to your entire life won't be able to see you vision and come along for the ride. It doesn't mean you have to eliminate them from your life, but it does mean you have to put boundaries in place about what sort of messaging you will and won't allow them to contribute to your life.

To build a dream life you must stop living according to family or societal pressure. You must pay attention to your inner compass and consult with only those who hold your same values and drive. How do we shake off the shackles of societal expectations? How do we put a stop to the family pressure and constant asking, "are you seeing anyone?"—as if your worth is measured by whether or not another person wants to spend time with you. How do you say no to someone you care for, but who isn't able to celebrate your success because they worry about you outlearning them? How do you say no to the father of your children when society tells you single parent households aren't good for kids?

It comes down to trust in the co-creation process. When a woman is connected to her Creator she knows she has everything inside her necessary to determine if a person is right for her or not. Trust in yourself is self-love. Sometimes, our trauma gets in the way of that connection so we need to heal first, and then we can start listening. Once you heal from trauma you can more easily determine if the small voice you hear is a trauma response, or if it's truly your intuition—a conversation with you God—about the right steps for you

My biggest relationship mistake was not allowing myself to heal from the trauma of my parent's marriage and the infidelity. My broken heart was not about G, nor about any other man, it was about me not loving myself fully. In my young adult years, I spent all my time growing academically, stepping into my power as a thinker, a healer, and a woman. I was choosing me, but I neglected to uncover the reasons for my lack of trust in men. The mistake of not healing meant I was choosing men who offered less than the true, beautiful love I deserved.

Healing the sort of trauma that causes you to forget yourself and choose others instead requires professional support. This is why every Queen needs a mental health professional as part of her Queendom. It is not your fault that you forget to choose you sometimes—based on the pressure women get to be and do all the things society says they should it makes sense that you forget about you.

Through therapy I learned to create a safe space for the hurt little girl inside me who craved true love from a man. Instead of looking for a hero who lived according to their values, stayed true to their promises, and wanted to build a dream with me, I became my own hero.

In becoming my own hero I released the anger and resentment that held me back from a strong relationship with Papi. I learned to see the truth. Papi was still my father. He was steady, present, loving, and supportive. He was not a good husband, but that didn't make him less of a father. I learned to forgive myself for staying stuck in the dirty chair of resentment and anger.

I learned to forgive Mami for putting up with Papi's infidelity and see that she was living her life according to rule she learned from those around her. Instead of taking on her pain I allowed it to inspire me to choose me and love me more than any other person could.

I also learned to forgive the younger Soribel who chose men who were not worthy of my affection. I healed the shame and embarrassment of being a single mom. I learned I had the tools, support, and wisdom to raise a successful Black man without a partner. I knew I could raise a son who knew how to love his partner well while building dreams together.

Chapter Takeaways

❖ Building an unbreakable life requires you to stop adhering to societal and family pressures and start living according to your inner compass.

❖ Forgiveness is for yourself, not for others.

❖ When practicing forgiveness, don't forget to forgive yourself.

❖ Healing the sort of trauma that causes you to forget yourself and choose others instead requires professional support.

❖ Trust in yourself and in the co-creative process is self-love.

Self-Evaluation Prompts

❖ What anger and resentment are you holding on to? Who are you angry with?

❖ How does that anger feel in your body?

❖ What is your anger keeping you from? How is it blocking you from creating the life you truly deserve?

❖ How would you feel if you could live without that anger and resentment?

❖ How would you think? How would you behave? What life would you create?

Part 4

More Passion, Less Perfection

I didn't sign a contract for perfection, I am committed to fulfilling my purpose with passion in my soul.

Chapter 9

Building a Successful Business

Fall in love with your life and business so much that it feels like you're living pure poetry.

At seven years old, I lay on my back under a Dominican sky, insects chirping around me. Without city lights, the stars took on their full power, shining down and illuminating bits of my world. As a young girl, I spent many nights like this, gazing at the stars, counting as high as possible, and naming the brightest ones. One night, as I lay with my hands behind my head, watching the heavens and a dream came to me. Not the abstract dream of a sleeping mind, but the fully awake daydream of a conscious mind unconstrained by the trials of life. At that moment, I knew I wanted to be a business owner, make people's lives better, and make a positive impact on the world. I also wanted to write a book.

I prayed to God, "Please let me experience something in my life I can write a book about."

I don't think my seven-year-old self knew what she was doing with that prayer. God certainly heard it, though. I've experienced enough to write many books about my life. Maybe young Soribel should have asked for a little bit less. While I've certainly had some trials, they really are just part of life. We can build a dream no matter what befalls us. My dream came from within me. Though it was influenced by Papi being a businessman and seeing others struggle, the true form of that dream came to me when I was alone, quiet, and enjoying the world God created for me.

I lost my dream somewhere along the way. Maybe I lost it after Papi immigrated or while we lived with Aunt Anna. I think it became partially buried under religious trauma and feelings of unworthiness. After moving to the United States, I had glimpses of it when I knew education was my route to success. Still, it was never as straightforward as that night in the Dominican with the grass tickling my bare legs and the nighttime breeze drifting over my skin.

I think that's the way it is with dreams—you get a sense of your purpose on this Earth when you're young and unconstrained by reality, and it seems so clear. Perhaps you danced around your bedroom singing and dreamed of creating music. Maybe you spent your free time lost in books or writing countless stories and dreaming of using words to connect people with their imaginations and the rest of the world. For me, the dream was entrepreneurship and helping others. We start with a firm sense of who we are. We feel no embarrassment about our goals and produce plays, songs, or stories, create towers out of blocks and call for others to look at our impressive accomplishments. And, often, they celebrate alongside us, encouraging us to continue dreaming. But then life happens, and our dream becomes just a bit less focused—cloudy, with a chance of a hurricane.

I struggled with acculturating, had trouble completing college courses due to language barriers, dealt with religious trauma, quit medical school, and then found what I hoped was love, only to find myself a single mother. I lost a child and trusted doctors to perform a life-threatening surgery on my brain. In 2017, I found myself working as a school social worker and struggling to provide for my son and me. I still knew what my dream was, but the path there no longer seemed like a highway. Anytime I thought of becoming a business owner, the course seemed a bit like a rutted dirt road so overgrown only one car could pass at a time. The overgrowth and intense turns meant that from where I stood, the end of the road seemed so far away that it might not have existed. I was allowing life to happen to me because taking control seemed impossible. I was exhausted, broke, and didn't see a way out.

I worked for people whose leadership didn't fit my values every day. I worked in a bilingual school and loved helping my community. I loved working with the children and assisting parents in connecting resources to create a better life. But the administration was full of people seeking to improve their lives and line their pockets without regard for the impact on others. I needed a way out.

At home, I couldn't find a way to make ends meet. At the time, John Anthony was in private school, and many people told me that was the problem—that I needed to stop paying tuition. But I knew before I became a mother that my children would have access to the same private education I enjoyed. My son's education was in line with my values of learning, education, and organizing knowledge in practical ways to help accomplish goals. John Anthony also enjoyed sports, music lessons, and other enrichment opportunities I wanted him to have. I didn't want to tell my boy he had to give up the things he loved because I couldn't make enough money. I needed a way to increase my earning capacity. I couldn't let go of my dreams or lower my expectations. We are given one life—one chance at making a difference in this world. When you have a dream, you have to do everything within your power to make it a reality.

That June, I sat at my dining room table feeling alone and losing hope. I lifted up my go-to prayer, "God, show me the path. My financial situation is difficult. Show me what to do. Put the resources and the people who will help me in my path, and I promise to do my part."

This is my favorite prayer, and it works every time. Whether I need more money, a medical miracle, a way to expand my business, a marketing strategy, or a donor for JC Precious Mind Foundation. When I need help from my co-creator, I pray, and then I get quiet. After lifting up that prayer, I sat at my dining table in quiet meditation because turning inward always yields the most powerful learning. I meditated for quite some time. Then, I heard a whisper, so quiet I almost missed it.

"You are sitting on gold."

I was confused. I was sitting on an oak dining chair and surrounded by bills I was struggling to pay. I was most definitely not sitting on gold. I had a decision to make. I could dismiss the notion, ignore that whisper and keep struggling, or I could lean in, stay quiet and see where it led me. I stayed in that chair.

"Go. Get your license and open your business. This is the time."

You see, the loud noises of the world tend to want to quiet the all-knowing voice inside—the one who wants to guide you and show you the path toward your purpose-driven dreams. Most of us miss the guidance because we can't stand being quiet enough to hear the soft, loving voice that lets us know exactly what we need at any given moment.

Then, my logical brain took over and tried to reason why this was a good time. John Anthony was older, and summer off was no longer the draw it had been when I accepted the position with the school system. Mami was living with me now and could support me in certain ways—offering childcare and taking care of the home. I decided it was time to take inspired and massive action to move forward and start a private therapy practice so I could serve clients in the way I thought best.

I needed to figure out the next step. A singular action I could take to move forward in the right direction. I sat there, staying quiet, focusing internally, and working through the list.

I already had all the practice hours that I needed for licensure.

I already had my necessary supervision hours.

If I wanted to open a private practice, the next step was a licensure exam.

I hadn't taken the exam for various reasons—my language barrier was certainly one of them—but mostly, I had a different path in mind. I saw myself doing more coaching than therapy in a private practice setting. Now, sitting in my dining room with a pile of bills to pay and John Anthony's school tuition due in August, I realized that private therapy practice would allow me to step into coaching while providing additional income for my family and broadening my impact on the community. Starting a private therapy practice was necessary for me to achieve what I'd dreamed of since I was seven years old, lying under the Dominican sky.

I needed to prepare for the exam. To motivate myself, I registered for an exam five weeks out. Then, I searched for a preparation program that met my needs. The one I found was perfect—it covered all the needed material, had a 95% passing rate, and gave you a step-by-step plan for preparing to pass the exam. The program gave practice questions and exams. It also taught self-care for test-taking like what to eat the morning of the exam, how to prepare the night before, and items to bring to boost energy during the test. There was just one problem. I couldn't afford the program. Supporting a household with only my income from the school district was proving impossible.

When people face that sort of barrier—especially a financial one—they often throw up their hands in defeat. They think they just have to put the dream away for now and return to it when they have more money. But that isn't how dreams work.

No dream will ever chase you down and tell you, "Now is the time." *We* must decide that now is the time. Then, even if we have to detour, we must take inspired and massive action.

I contacted the creator of the preparation program, explained my situation, and asked for a payment plan. They could say no, and I'd have to find another path, but I'd detoured before. When they responded by offering a payment plan I could fit into my budget, I got started immediately. I went through the course material and created a five-week plan to prepare myself for the exam.

You see, you should never get defeated before you even try. You must decide that it will work for you no matter what. Your faith and trust will carry you through. When we allow ourselves to think negatively, that it won't work, then we tend to manifest exactly what we are asking for. Instead of focusing your energy on why things won't work out, keep your mind on positive outcomes so you can manifest what you want.

That summer, I didn't spend lazy days on the beach like my friends from the school district. I didn't spend the time with John Anthony I had in previous summers. Instead, I set up a classroom at my dining room table. I woke each morning, and Mami looked after John Anthony, never minding her Abuela role. She cooked and cleaned around me, and took my boy to the park and on outings. I sat in my chair studying as if it were my full-time job. I quite literally could not afford to fail this test.

You see, when your only choice is winning, you will win. Your winning attitude will carry you through because winners will never lose. When you don't get the results you desire, you have two options. You can see it as a failure. Or you can see that as feedback so you can adjust, refine, reorganize, or try a different strategy.

The exam day came, and I walked in knowing I had the standard four hours plus an additional two hours offered to bilingual students with language barriers. I expected to take all six hours to complete the exam. I sat at my desk, pencil poised, and opened the test. When I closed it and looked at the clock, I realized only an hour had passed. I immediately felt anxious. Did I rush? Did I not answer the questions fully? I reviewed my answers but found none I wished to change. I even looked for parts of the test I overlooked my first time through. There were none.

I completed the exam in an hour. When I clicked complete on my test, the proctors raised their eyebrows and asked if I was sure I was finished. I nodded, and they processed my exam for scoring. The results were instant. I passed the exam and was now a licensed social worker capable of opening my own practice. I started that school year knowing I wouldn't finish it. I couldn't wait to begin seeing clients, but I didn't have a space or platform for doing so. So, like I always do, I reached out to my support system. A friend of mine ran a private practice and allowed me to begin seeing clients as an independent contractor. This was the beginning of me reclaiming my space in the world and reconnecting to the work I wanted to do.

Working in the schools fulfilled me in many ways and provided a sense of security with benefits, a pension, and a regular paycheck that I craved as I raised a young son. Our needs as a family, however, outgrew what it could provide. As a school social worker, I enjoyed helping the children and families of the bilingual school where I worked. I enjoyed seeing the children's progress and connecting families with resources in the community, but I felt I needed to do more. I needed my own space to work with clients in the ways I thought best. I wanted to offer more than the school district allowed.

After a few weeks, I started SMPsychotherapy and Counseling Services. I didn't have an office. I didn't have administrative staff. I didn't have a telehealth platform. What I did have was a waitlist. Potential clients craved a bilingual therapist with my credentials and experience. I found a therapist willing to rent her office space to me for $20 per session. This ate into my reimbursement rates but was necessary to help the number of people I wanted to reach. I also saw clients in their homes. I thought I'd continue like this for a few months—working at the school during the day and seeing clients in the evenings and on weekends. It soon became clear I couldn't do that.

My waitlist grew, and I began to see possibilities. I knew I needed to leave my job with the school district and launch my private practice full-time. Friends and family cautioned me. How could I leave my steady paycheck? How could I give up the summers off with John Anthony? How would I make up for the pension the school district offered? My friends and family didn't mean to suffocate my dreams—they were scared and worried about me and allowed that fear to take over. I couldn't let their fear become mine. I needed to stick with the voice within—the conversations I had with my co-creator about my purpose, my passion, and my goals.

Sticking with your purpose isn't always easy. Like my friends and family, I feared taking the leap to business owner-ship. Rather than listen to all those saying I couldn't or shouldn't jump, I reached out to a friend who is a single mom and a suc-cessful business owner. When you're building a dream, the peo-ple you listen to matter—choose people who will encourage you.

"I'm afraid to leave my job. What if it doesn't work, and I fail and don't have that stable income anymore?"

"Afraid or not, all you have to do is decide to do it. Let's say you fail; what's the worst that happens? You have God to help you out."

"Yes, but John Anthony depends on me."

Cindy wasn't letting me sit in my fear, "Rather than think about what happens if it doesn't work, think about what could happen if it does. How will that feel?"

I wanted to find my own office space but worried I'd be unable to pay rent each month. My inner voice was once again drowned out by external noise. I needed more encouragement. I spoke with a dear friend who encouraged me to jump to the next level.

"God has taken you to this point. You think he will leave you now?" she asked, eyebrows raised, "Girl, jump, the worse that could happen is that it does not work. But what if it does work? Then what?"

Often our fear tells us it's too hard and we're going to fail. It tells us we can't and shouldn't. Fear couldn't stop me because I decided my son needed a better education. He wasn't going to be a statistic. I was going to provide everything he needed to be successful. When society told me children of single mothers have problems, I chose to be the parent my son needed—the provider he needed. I couldn't let fear control my life. You can't let fear overpower you, either. Instead, journal and meditate on success. What if your plan works? What if you have the right support? What if you get the knowledge you need to be success-ful? How will success feel? How would you behave? How would you think if it did work? These questions have often pulled me through when my mind wants to play tricks or create negative narratives about my reality.

Fear is going to be present when you do something new. You are out of your comfort zone. Fear is telling you you're ready to step into an unknown space. It's telling you you're prepared to do things you've never done. You're ready to believe in yourself and leap because you're guided by your Creator. You will have plenty of fear every time you make a decision for your business. Decide anyway. Your greatest success is on the other side of fear. Acting in the face of fear creates power and greater opportunities and helps you grow mentally and spiritually. That energy of success trickles down to every area of your life. So, expect to be afraid, acknowledge your fear when it pops up, then pray for guidance from your co-creator. When a woman prays for guidance from her co-creator, she always gets to where she's going.

When I feel afraid, it is because my vision, dreams, and goals are big. If I am dreaming, visualizing, or setting goals and they don't make me feel a bit afraid, I know they are not big enough. I know that I am not being stretched enough. Fear can also be a sign of excitement and a sign of the amazing things that could be manifested in your life and business.

The day I handed in my notice at work just a couple months after the school year started, I truly stepped into my power. When I walked out of my supervisor's office and got a phone call from Human Resources begging me to reconsider, offering me a transfer to a different school, or other perks, I declined. Saying no to the school district was empowering. This was not about money, a comfortable office, or any other small comfort. This was about leaning into my purpose.

Within a month, my continuously growing waitlist made it clear that I could not continue in private practice solo. I needed to open a group therapy practice. I offered employment opportunities to other therapists wanting to make enough money to support their families. This was the beginning of a group therapy practice that grew by 2022 to include over twenty-plus therapists and a few psychiatric mental health nurse practitioners. I've leveraged my success in a private group practice to expand services and reach more people. I added book writing and became a best-selling author, launched my business coaching and consulting programs, found public speaking opportunities, became an associate professor at Post University, and a concierge sex therapist and coach. I've also secured over 150k in donations for JC Precious Mind Foundation so we can help more special needs children in the Dominican Republic meet their potential.

Deciding to start my business as a struggling single mom was the one push I needed to keep on moving forward. That decision was all it took. My son wasn't a reason I couldn't start a business. He was the reason I needed and desired to. As a single parent, I could cry because I don't have co-parent support, or I could take the energy I'd spend being sad and angry and channel it into power and purpose. I could stress over how to pay bills or use that creative energy to write a business plan.

When I started this process, I did not do it alone. I went back to the foundation of my strength. I used my prayer. I got quiet at my dining room table and prayed. I stayed there, quiet until I heard the guidance of my co-creator. I relied on journaling and meditation to work through my fears and help find detours when I faced a roadblock. Any time I felt blocked or afraid of moving forward, I returned to that prayer.

"God, show me the path. I am willing to do my part."

We cannot look outside ourselves to achieve our dreams and work in alignment with our purpose. We can't poll social media or ask our parents what they think we should do. There is so much noise coming from society telling us who to be, what to do, and what will make us worthy of love. It is easy to get lost in that noise—we live in fear of judgment and get sucked into living the life we think we should instead of the life we were created to live. When the noise gets loud enough, it can drown out our inner wisdom until it's barely a whisper.

Quiet reflection is where we reconnect with that voice. When you silence your mind, eliminate the external noise, and keep your body still, that voice grows louder when you make time to stop being busy. You will know your true purpose if you listen to this inner wisdom. Your purpose is the dream that fills you with energy (and a bit of fear because getting out of our comfort zone is always scary). That excitement is the energy you felt as a child when you knew your purpose and were unconstrained by reality and societal pressure.

Think about finding your purpose like this. If you drive home, park your car, walk to your front door with your keys in your hand, unlock the door, and set your things down in the entryway, you know your keys are inside the house. You used them to open the door. When you need to leave the house in the morning, you aren't going to run outside and look in your car for the keys because you know they are inside. When you lose parts of yourself—love for yourself, understanding who you are, knowledge of your true purpose, where do you look?

So many of us ask family and friends or poll others. "What do you think I should major in? Should I apply for that new job? Do you think I have what it takes to start a business?" Stop asking those questions of the people around you. Stop scrolling on Instagram and stop watching other people set up a life like the one you crave and feeling jealous that you don't have the luxuries they enjoy. Stop looking outside for the keys—you know they're inside.

Once that voice grows loud enough, it's time to take inspired, massive action. The universe is working in your favor. Your co-creator is ready to guide you. You must do your part and take the first step to move toward your goal. Your first step can be big or small as long as it aligns with your purpose. Motivation to continue will follow that first action, and soon those actions will build on one another. You'll create an action plan for the step-by-step process to get you to your goal. This plan is a roadmap to your dreams, desires, and business.

Your roadmap will change. It's a common assumption that any interruption to your plan is negative—but sometimes, the things that change your plan and cause you to detour are positive developments. I thought I'd work as a solo provider when I began my business. I soon realized that to have the impact I wanted, I needed to switch to a group practice model. The path to success involves being open to detours and having the flexibility to adjust the course when needed.

A few months into my entrepreneurial journey, I had a revelation. When I worked in the school district for people whose values didn't match mine—people who were more interested in personal accomplishments and financial gain than in helping the students we were meant to serve—I shrunk. My skills were not properly put to use, and they waned. When I stepped into my power and reclaimed my place as a therapist and an entrepreneur, I realized I had the potential to have even more impact than I dreamed. Working according to my own values and building my legacy instead of someone else's made showing up to work every day easier. I was fulfilled, I was empowered, and I was excited to see what I could create.

Now, my business offers employment opportunities that allow other therapists to support their families while providing mental health care that so many need. I created a workplace where I treat employees as collaborators, help them expand their knowledge, and support their goals. My dreams keep growing to include coaching and expanding SMPsychotherapy to other states. My financial goals get bigger every time my impact goals do.

As women, it's often hard for us to step into leadership. Society tells us we get what we get, and we shouldn't ask for more, much less demand it. We are taught women are caretakers and that we exist to serve others. When we step into greater spaces, we should apologize for what we desire and create. You don't have to apologize because your purpose is stronger than any societal pressure to remain small. Do not let someone else tell you your worth or dictate what you can achieve.

Don't listen to the people who tell you wanting success is selfish. Being a woman who wants more doesn't take away from the world. On the contrary, when good women are successful, they reach out to other women and build them up. God gave you gifts so you could share them with the world. When women work in alignment with their purpose, they respect others' abilities and worth. They are not merely lining their own pockets. In addition to serving the community and offering employment opportunities, SMPsychotherapy allowed me to fund JC's Precious Minds Foundation and improve the lives of single mothers and their special needs children in the Dominican Republic. The foundation also seeks to help moms complete their education or start a small business.

And what about that fear? I feared I wouldn't be able to make this dream a reality. The nagging voice said I couldn't provide the stability I needed and enjoy a few of the luxuries I wanted. As a business owner, I give myself the same stability I had in the school system: paychecks every two weeks, a pension, and healthcare. But now I have an added bonus—I have the time to do the important things. Since starting my own business, I've never had to miss John Anthony's school performances or felt pulled between working set hours to make money for someone else and being the mother my son needs. I give myself time for the things that matter. I take vacations, show up for family events, and never need to ask permission to do so. I became my own boss because I didn't need someone else telling me what to do to be successful. All the motivation, guidance, and redirection I need are within me.

Chapter Takeaways

❖ Always ask for guidance, then stay quiet and listen for the answer.

❖ Moving toward your purpose will not eliminate fear. You'll have plenty of fear. Do the thing anyway.

❖ The empowerment that comes from knowledge is bigger than any fear.

❖ You were created with a great purpose. Let that purpose guide your destiny.

Self-Evaluation Prompts

❖ Find a quiet space and dream for a moment. What did you want to do, be, or become when you were a child?

❖ Identify your favorite prayer to ask for guidance.

❖ What is one project, career, or business idea you would like to explore this year?

❖ What would it take for you to do, be, or become who you really want to be?

❖ Identify people who can support you and resources you can learn from.

❖ Identify the first step of the ladder to your dreams, desires, and purpose.

Chapter 10

Eight Pillars of Business Success

A successful business requires unbreakable energy,
a growth mindset, and proven strategies.

When I'm giving a keynote speech about building a business or even sharing in online spaces, people ask me, "Soribel, how do I get started? How do I grow my business into something sustainable and profitable?"

I can wax poetic about how all the answers lie within you, and if you know your purpose and live in alignment, you'll find your way, but people often want or need some more concrete guidance than that. During an annual review of my business success and planning for growth I realized that there was a need for successful private practice owners to show other practices how to grow and scale their businesses.

I began offering business coaching in 2021 and launched SMBusiness Coaching and Consulting. I certainly couldn't have built my business without support from other successful business owners, and this is my chance to share my learning with you so your path to entrepreneurial success is more streamlined. In 2022 SMPsychotherapy and Counseling Services grew over 89% using the strategies for organized knowledge, personal development, business planning, and effective strategies I'll share with you in this chapter.

In 2004, long before I started SMPsychotherapy and Counseling Services, I returned to school for a master's in business administration. I was far from starting my own business— I was wading through the early career of a social worker. But getting that degree was my way of honoring the little girl who dreamed under the Dominican stars of a business career. I knew entrepreneurship was my destination, and I knew I needed business knowledge to make it happen. Inspired by Papi's career and no longer constrained by the rules of the Pentecostal church, I felt free to expand my learning.

When I meet with coaching clients who wish to start or grow their own businesses they often lament their lack of a business degree. While I have a business degree, that isn't why I'm successful. Plenty of people without business degrees create empires that employ thousands, make an enormous positive impact in our world, and stay true to their values. So how do you build a business without a business degree? To create your entrepreneurship dream, you will need the ability to identify your knowledge gaps and the willingness to seek information to fill in those gaps. Once you have the information, you need to organize your knowledge into useful, practical steps to advance your goals.

This chapter fills in what formal education often fails to teach us—the steps for starting a business. You want to live a life of your own design, and, for many, starting a business is the path they choose.

These principles don't just apply to business. Use them to evaluate and change your life at home, the structure of your days, or the way you engage with your career. In the following pages, when I say business, you can easily substitute career, household, or relationship.

Identify Knowledge Gaps

In business, knowing what you *don't* know is more important than anything you *do* know. The capacity to identify your knowledge gaps represents a willingness to learn and grow and an ability to remain flexible. I didn't use my MBA immediately after finishing it because I spent years building experience in social work first. Even business owners with degrees must engage in lifelong learning to ensure success. When I opened my private practice, I had quite a few knowledge gaps and a lot to learn. Those knowledge gaps led to fears, and that fear threatened to stop me before I even began.

Starting a business is an exercise in overcoming fear. The biggest fear I experienced was the fear of success. Now that I know more about business, I realize this is a common fear for many entrepreneurs. We worry about what we will do if we achieve our dreams and what we must strive for next. We worry about how others might respond to our success. For me, deeply ingrained religious trauma caused me to fear success because my subconscious still held onto the idea that success and wealth were sinful. I feared that if I tapped into the level of success I wanted, it would change who I was and make me a bad person. I worried that seeking success would make me unworthy of a relationship with God. I needed something to turn off that fear. Knowledge is the antidote to fear, so figuring out what you need to learn is the first step in building a successful business. After passing the licensing exam, I needed to learn about credentialing with insurance companies, the legal aspects of working with clients, how to attract new clients, and a host of other business principles. My need for new learning continues as my business expands and the need for mental health care evolves.

You will encounter fear as you start your business and even years into the process. Remember that knowledge is the antivenom and seek it. Identify what you need to learn to start your business by studying other businesses, listening to podcasts, reading books, and/or working with a business coach or consultant. Every time you learn something new, it should lead to more questions and identifying other things you want to learn. Make a to-learn list in your journal. All of these knowledge gaps become part of your business action plan—the steps you need to take to move toward success. You will need to learn as you go, implement new practices, and regularly adjust when you learn something new. When you make your action plan for starting your business, it's easy to feel overwhelmed by how much you don't know. So, when you identify knowledge gaps, moving quickly to the next step to stave off overwhelm is vital.

Seek New Learning

Looking for opportunities to learn what you don't know about business is exciting and a bit daunting. Don't try to learn everything at once. Once you have a list created, prioritize it. What do you need to learn first? What can wait until later? Take your prioritized list and identify ways to learn. Be open to reprioritizing your list often.

When I started my business and made my list of knowledge gaps, I decided to hire support to help me learn. I hired a business coach to guide me through practical business creation steps. I found a life coach to help me with imposter syndrome, limiting beliefs about success, and other personal roadblocks. I also sought camaraderie with a mentor—someone in my field who was doing what I wanted to do. I kept regular appointments with my therapist when I needed emotional support.

New learning doesn't have to come from coaches, although I've found working with coaches to be worth every penny. The support is personalized, and I can focus only on filling in my knowledge gaps. In addition to coaching, I took courses. I found courses about aspects of business I needed to learn and dealing with the fear of success. I also sought new knowledge in self-development books and books by people whose entrepreneurial journey inspired me. When you're engaged in these learning activities do not simply read and listen passively. Study them like you're in college. Take notes, re-write notes, highlight the important concepts, organize your notes, and revisit them as needed. That knowledge assuaged my fear of success and allowed me to lean into entrepreneurship. I learned that being successful meant having the impact I always dreamed of—the more people I helped, the more successful I became. My success, then, is not selfish.

When I wasn't working with my coach or taking courses, I read books, listened to podcasts, and watched motivational videos online. I joined supportive communities and attended conferences, seminars, and business retreats. This constant flow of new information gives entrepreneurs the energy they need to continue building our empires and impacting the world. Knowledge energy is to entrepreneurship like fuel is to a car. You need the energy and knowledge to continue. If you buy a car, even a beautiful red Mercedes convertible, you cannot ask to drive without gasoline. It does not matter how expensive, luxurious, beautiful, and amazing that vehicle is. It doesn't matter if you beg, cajole, or demand. Without energy that car will not move toward the destination. Without knowledge, an entrepreneur cannot move toward their dream. You need energy. You can find your energy sources from spiritual, emotional, intellectual, and mental support.

What do you need to learn? Start a list on your desktop or in a notebook you'll use only for business development. This list will grow because the more you learn about business, the more questions you'll have. Revisit this list often, and prioritize it. Each time you visit the list, ask yourself what the next thing you need to learn about to advance toward your goals is.

Organize Knowledge into Useful Steps

Knowledge is power. Organized knowledge is power and freedom. When you take in new information, it can feel a bit scattered. As a business owner, you may understand you need to create a structure for taxes, hiring new staff, and marketing. Without organizing that knowledge into a useful structure, it's just a pile of things you know—good for cocktail party conversation but not useful in the real world. When I started SMPsychotherapy and Counseling services, I knew I needed to organize all the information I learned in my MBA program, in my years of providing therapy, and in the coaching and coursework so I could use it to create something tangible. That's why I created my Million Dollar Elements for Business Success. In this chapter, I'll walk you through an overview of the steps I take with each of my coaching clients—the same steps I used to build SMpsychotherpay and the steps I use every time I want to grow my business further.

The Million Dollar Elements for Business Success include Personal Development, Business Mindset, and Business Planning. Your business plan is essential for success and includes business structure, business model, marketing, business finance, and systems and supports.

Personal Development

The first pillar of business success is to engage in continuous personal development. Your business will reflect you—your strengths, your weaknesses, your values, and your limiting beliefs. To start your personal development plan, take time to learn about yourself through a self-assessment. A self-assessment is a tool to help you identify potential growth areas in your life. Identify where you are now in terms of family, career, friends, finances, and self-care (health, fun, lifestyle). Then, evaluate how you got where you are. What action or inaction helped you become who you are today? How satisfied are you with the current shape of your life in each area on a scale of 1-10? Then, imagine where you want to be. Where do you want your business to be? Your relationships? Your family life? How will you feel once you have the life you want? How will your thought patterns change?

The areas where you aren't satisfied are areas of personal development. For each category in your life where your satisfaction rating is low, identify one thing you can do to move to the next level. You don't have to attack every area at once. Pick one or two you're most dissatisfied with and create goals around those areas. For example, if you rated finances as the lowest level of satisfaction, you might set a goal to earn an additional $10,000 this year. If your lowest satisfaction is around self-care, your goal might be to include a ten-minute walk once a day, or to schedule one fun evening out per month.

Make sure your goals are realistic and achievable, but don't make them so easy that you don't have to change anything about your life to reach them. I like to set goals that stretch, scare and excite me. You want to expand your capacity to create. The goal here is to change, grow, and create your level-10 life. The goal should also have action steps, a timeline for the completion of each step, and a list of the resources you'll need to move you into alignment with your purpose and goal.

The more your actions align with your values, the closer you are to living your true purpose and the more satisfied you will feel about your life. Maybe you need to read about time management or learn to disconnect from electronics and be present with your children when you're home. Seek help from a therapist, a life coach, self-development books, online courses, and conversations with people who are living a life similar to the one you want.

Only share your vision, goals, dreams, and actions with those who are also in alignment with growth and expansion. Sharing your goals with a scarcity-minded person is a waste of time and energy. Share with those that will push, encourage and challenge you to go for it—those who are part of your supportive circle.

Business Mindset

The second pillar of business success is to engage in building a strong business mindset. Think of your business as a house. When a builder starts, they choose where to build. They may have many areas to choose from—a sunny beachfront, a spot at the edge of a wild forest, or a condo complex in the city center. Where you build matters. When you're an entrepreneur, your mindset about business is the location of your house. If you build on sand, the first storm will wash your house away. If you take the time to dig deep into the earth and construct a solid foundation, your house will withstand decades of storms and hurricanes. Your business mindset can determine how success-ful you become. With the right mindset, your business will have a strong foundation to expand and grow. With the right mind-set, you can build a Queendom.

Entrepreneurship requires you to have a growth mindset that views talent, ability, and intelligence as things you can im-prove through well-placed effort. A growth mindset says, "I can always learn more. When I fail, it's really just a growth oppor-tunity." A growth mindset sets you up for self-reflection, con-stant improvement, and lifelong learning. If you come to your entrepreneurial journey with a fixed mindset that sees skills and smarts as unchangeable regardless of time or effort, you won't allow yourself to learn the skills necessary to succeed. A fixed mindset will keep you stuck. The great thing about mindset is that it can change if you do the work. The strategies I use for developing and keeping a growth mindset are the same I use for learning any skill or information: seek support, read, listen to courses, and network.

In addition to a growth mindset, you also need to have the mindset of a business owner, not the mindset of an em-ployee or helper. In social work, we are taught how to be helpers. We learn how to identify mental health issues, connect clients to community resources, and network with other social workers. There are no classes in most social work programs about how to build a business. This is true for most helping professions— nurses, teachers, and other helping professionals are taught how to care for others, but not how to use their skills in an entrepreneurial space to broaden their impact and increase their financial health. During my social work programs, however, I had the mindset of someone who wanted to be in business. It made other social workers and colleagues around me uncomfortable. How dare I talk about business *and* the helping profession?!? We got into this profession to help people. Yes, everyone is in the helping business, we just help people directly or indirectly. We are all servers. I started developing that mindset at seven years old and never stopped. This mindset often meant I clashed with my peers and instructors. If I focused on increasing impact and building a profitable business, how could I say that my main purpose was helping others?

These people had a helper mindset—not a business mindset. If you're walking into entrepreneurship, you need a business mindset. A business mindset says that your time and skills are worth massive compensation and that by increasing your reach, you can build a successful, profitable business and help more people improve their lives. This is one of the main reasons people get stuck in business and lack growth. You can't build a castle with the same tools you build a small house on the sand.

Building the right mindset for business success involves the following steps:

❖ Know exactly what you desire in your business.

❖ Identify the impact you want your business to generate.

❖ Understand how you want to feel in your business and the great work you want to do in the world.

❖ Know how you would want to think as a business owner and how you would like to think about success.

❖ Describe how you would behave as a successful business owner.

Successful people feel, think, behave and have different results compared to those who do not have the right mindset.

This exercise for developing your business mindset is the first step to shaping the mindset you need to create your dream life. Business success is not just about the revenue you want to generate, taxes, staff, support, etc. It's also about the energy you bring to your business and converting that energy into a positive impact on the world.

Business Plan

The third step to building your entrepreneurial dreams is a comprehensive business plan. If your business mindset is the foundation of your entrepreneurial journey, and organized knowledge propels you forward, then a business plan is the blueprint for the entire structure. Creating a business plan requires you to make decisions about every aspect of your business. These decisions are essential, but they are not permanent. You can change your business plan at any time as you grow and learn.

Your business plan should include your mission statement and vision. A vision includes your current and future objectives. The mission includes a description of the business and how you plan to serve your clients. The mission and vision serve as a guidepost pointing you and any employees you have in the direction of success. They also help potential clients determine if you're the right company for them.

In your business plan, take time to detail your ideal clients or customers. Include demographics such as age, income level, profession, and location, but don't stop there. Detail your ideal clients' emotions and the problems your services and products can help them solve.

Your business plan must also include goals for your business. Make your goals SMART: Specific, Measurable, Achievable, Realistic, and Time-Based. Having goals for one, three, six, twelve-month and five-year intervals is also a great idea.

Specific: Rather, than "I will fill my caseload," try "I will serve 20 clients." Being specific allows for better reflection on goal achievement and planning for the future.

Measurable: Your goal should include a measurable outcome. In the statement, "I will serve 20 clients," adding "each week" makes it easier to measure success. If you're only serving 15 clients a week, but have 20 clients total, you've not met your goal yet.

Attainable: Your goal should fit into the time constraints without taking away from the time you need to complete back-office tasks. If you only have time for 15 clients a week when you account for office work and your personal life, set your goal accordingly!

Relevant: Your goals should relate directly to your mission and vision. If the goal doesn't fit into your long-term plans—get rid of it! You don't have time for distracting dribs and drabs as a business owner.

Time-Based: Stating that you want to serve 20 clients a week is great, but in long-term planning, you want to set goals with an end date in mind to help you adjust marketing efforts, set up systems and processes, etc. "I will serve 20 clients a week within six months of opening my business" is a long-term goal that will allow you to track progress, adjust your efforts, and reflect as you go.

Another critical component of your business plan is continuing education. An entrepreneurial journey requires lifelong learning. Detail any certifications you want to pursue, or courses you plan to take. The other components of your business plan are more detailed and require in-depth information. I've outlined each part in the next sections.

Business Structure

When SMPsychotherapy started, and my waitlist was longer than my list of to-do's, I quickly realized I needed to make some decisions about business finances and accounting. I also realized I needed more knowledge about both of those things. I hired an accountant, Antonio, and set up a meeting with him at a coffee shop between our offices. As we sat across from each other, caffeine cooling in front of us, Antonio detailed what he'd learned about my business from the documents I sent him.

"You are not paying yourself enough."

"But I have all these expenses for the business."

"If you don't pay yourself from your business, you will pay more in taxes."

Antonio went on to explain the differences between an LLC and an S corp. We discussed why an S corp was the right structure for my business and how paying myself a salary would lower my overall taxes and ensure I could continue to expand my business the way I wanted.

The more we talked, the more panic set in. How could I ensure I had enough to cover payroll, insurance, and other business expenses if I paid myself a salary? Would I be able to save for retirement? Fear took hold because this new milestone happened faster than I expected. That speed made me nervous. Getting out of your comfort zone is always terrifying. That fear signaled to me that I had an opportunity to learn and grow.

During that initial meeting, Antonio and I went over tax laws and implications for my business. I decided to become an S corp and hired Antonio for three reasons: 1) He came highly recommended. 2) He had the services I needed. 3) The confidence he had during our meeting. Over the next several months, I worked with Antonio to learn as much as possible about the different business structures to make informed decisions about SMPsychotherapy. With his guidance, I learned about sole proprietorships and partnerships. We reviewed everything I needed to know about payroll, tax implications and structure, and how to make sure I paid myself a living wage. Your business structures are the load-bearing walls of your house and the support beams that ensure it is built to last. Include them in your business plan to help guide your other decisions. Selecting the right business structure can help you ensure you meet all legal requirements and set your business up for the rate of growth you want.

To create a business structure that allows for growth, follow these steps:

❖ Based on your business plan, which business structure would support your goals and growth?

❖ If you don't have an accountant, identify who you will set a consultation with. (Hint most of them offer free consultations.) You can reach out to your network of friends in business. I am sure they will have a recommendation for you. I reached out to my network of other business owners and asked for a referral.

❖ When is your meeting with your new accountant?

❖ What documents do you need to provide him or her?

❖ Make a decision based on your meeting with your accountant and your research.

Business Model

Your business model is a part of your business plan that represents the services or products you want to offer the community you serve. There are three basic models, but many businesses are a combination of one or more models. You can set up a business-to-consumer model, a business-to-business model, or a Christian-based business model. You'll also make decisions about how you serve those clients.

When I first began, I thought I'd operate as a solo practitioner—I'd provide therapy services to clients whose insurance companies would pay me. But, the waitlist of potential clients clamoring for a bilingual therapist wouldn't allow for that small business-to-consumer model. I needed to open a group practice. That group practice would include employees and independent contractors. Shifting to a larger-scale business model tested my mindset once again. The same will probably be true for you.

Thinking bigger, doing something new, or changing your business's operations is scary because our brains are wired to keep the status quo. Your brain will tell you you are doing too much and dreaming too big. You'll think that staying small is the right decision and that you don't need to expand. Your brain is comfortable doing this thing you're good at—this thing that is now without knowledge gaps. You've done the learning, and now your brain wants to settle in for twenty years of sameness.

What's wrong with that? Well, if your purpose is to have a huge impact on the world and connect people with your products or services because you solve a problem, then this question isn't about you and your comfort level. It's about helping more people. Getting out of your comfort zone is required if you want to increase your reach.

To prompt myself to get out of my comfort zone in business I identify opportunities for growth using a SWOT analysis. I complete one with my private business and consulting clients. I do one for SMPsychotherapy every calendar year, or more often if it seems necessary. SWOT stands for Strengths, Weaknesses, Opportunities, and Threats. Analyzing these business components can help you find what your company does well, find opportunities for improvement, and identify potential growth areas. Analyzing your business in this way can help your strengths to address weaknesses and identify the next right area to invest time and money in for optimal growth. I also survey my current clients to find out what other services they need; such as psychiatric and med management services, support and group therapy, online courses, etc. Surveying my clients not only gives me an idea of other services needed but also helps me learn how satisfied they are with our services.

Your business model is not a fixed concept. It's merely a floorplan of your house. As your business changes, the business model you started with may require an addition or a repurposing of space. I started as a business-to-consumer solo practice, moved into group practice, and recently added a business-to-business portion that allows me to coach other entrepreneurs in their journey. Growth requires constant reflection and adaptation.

In the business model part of your business plan, detail your current model and what model you want your business to have a year from now and three years from now.

Business Marketing

You have a solid business mindset, structure, and model. Your house is structurally sound and operating well. Many people get to a point where the day-to-day operations of their busi-

ness run smoothly and wrongly assume they don't need to refine their strategies. The trouble with that assumption is that if
you don't maintain your house over the years it will eventually
crumble. The way to sustain your business is through marketing
efforts aligned with your mission and vision.

Many people wrongly assume that marketing is selfish
and that you're attempting to manipulate people into paying for
your product or service. Others feel bad for asking for the sale
or offering a service to someone who needs it. But that couldn't
be further from the truth. Ethical marketing practices connect
people who need your services with your company. If you're
afraid of marketing your business, take some time to tap into
where that fear comes from. Your customers are waiting for you
to offer the service and product they need so they can buy it
from you. They want you to find a solution to their problem.
The Latino community had been waiting for me to offer bilingual services.

When I first started SMPsychotherapy, I worried about
using social media to market my services. I worried people
would judge me as self-centered, so I held back. I let fear make
decisions for my business. Sure, I used therapy websites, and
some of our clients came directly from insurance companies we
paneled with, but I had clinicians with open spots in their sched-
ules. My mission was to help as many people as possible find
mental wellness so they could create the lives and relationships
they wanted. If I wanted to help more people, I needed to reach
them and tell them about our services.

Once I figured out where that fear came from, I needed
to dismantle it. I asked myself how I wanted to feel about marketing. The truth was I wanted to see marketing as a necessary
part of running a business and do it without fear of judgment.
Sometimes that means removing unsupportive or negative people from my social media connections. It always means that
even if I feel afraid about a post I want to publish, I need to publish it anyway. Once I got over fear referrals flowed in. One Facebook contact sent me ten new clients. Another woman sent
me eight clients. When I show up in marketing efforts, I now use
every avenue that is legal and ethical because expanding my
reach and growing my client base is how I achieve my mission.

In addition to overcoming the fear of social media or online marketing, I encourage you to use traditional marketing efforts. This could include print advertisements, or connecting with area businesses to look for partnership opportunities. There are so many other opportunities for transitional marketing to grow your business. SMPsychotherapy sends introduction letters and brochures to area doctor's offices. We send the package, follow up with a phone call, and then set an appointment to meet with the staff. In addition to print marketing, find ways to network where your ideal clients are or where the people who serve your clients spend time. Find conferences for your niche and go. Have business cards and brochures available and highlight the value you provide. Marketing is about connection. The more you connect, the faster you meet your goals and create the massive impact you desire.

As you create your marketing strategy, consider online and social media marketing efforts, but also include traditional marketing, such as partnering with businesses and using print advertisements. Like other sections, this part of your business plan will change as your business grows.

Consider the following questions for your marketing plan:

❖ Who do you want to target? (Think about age group, gender, profession, life stage, etc.)

❖ What do you want your hourly rate to be?

❖ Where will you offer your services or sell products? Will you have a location or work online only?

❖ What is the potential market for your business in your area?

❖ What existing services and products are already in the area you plan to cover?

❖ Is the marketplace crowded?

❖ What skills and professional credentials do you have or can you develop?

Business Finance

As women, we need to empower ourselves to cultivate financial knowledge. We must have an intimate relationship with our finances and look at things honestly. When I started my business all of the money mindset stuff I learned as a member of the Pentecostal Church crept in and threatened to derail me. My brain spun on old limiting beliefs such as "money doesn't grow on trees" and "people who seek wealth are bound to go to hell." I knew that I needed to fix my money mindset, just like my mindset about business growth.

When you're starting a business, you need to examine your personal financial patterns and behaviors. Ask yourself these questions:

❖ What were the stories you learned about money from your parents?

❖ Were they spenders?

❖ Were they excessively frugal?

❖ Did you grow up with a lack of resources?

❖ How did those early teachings about money shape how you behave around money now?

By working through these questions, I rephrased my belief about money.

Now, I see money as the energy that supports me and my vision. Money is meant to be spent, shared, saved, and invested. Money is a wonderful tool that allows me to hire other providers and therapists. Money allows those people to care for their families. Money is a tool that provides resources to children and their families in the Dominican Republic through JC's Precious Minds Foundation. Money unlocks access for business owners to expand opportunities, increase greatness, and provide resources.

Once you have a better emotional relationship with money, how do you manage it all? Never one to struggle alone when I can find support, I sought help from my CPA, Antonio. I used marketing to ensure a constant flow of clients so I could manage payroll, savings, training, and overhead expenses. I set up QuickBooks, though you may choose another financial management system. I organized everything coming into the business accounts and everything going out. I constantly reinvest in my business based on goals, current trends, and my vision for the future.

To get savvy about business finances, begin with these questions:

❖ How do you feel about money?

❖ What's your core belief about money?

❖ How did you learn your primary ideas and values about money?

❖ What spending patterns do you have? Are they healthy habits? What, if anything, do you wish to change?

❖ What resources can you use to learn more about managing and growing your money?

❖ What financial management software will you use for your business?

❖ Who can support you in your financial matters?

Systems and Support

The success of your business depends on the systems you put in place. These systems can streamline processes and procedures to save you time so you can work in your area of genius. Really, that's the point of all of this—business planning, structure, models, marketing, and financial wellness all allow you to spend as much time as possible doing the work you excel in because that's the route to profitability.

My genius is providing therapy services and teaching others how to create their entrepreneurial dreams. I do not spend my time working on payroll, billing insurance companies, or scheduling appointments. Instead, I leverage my time on money-making activities. I create opportunities for others who are more qualified in those areas to shine. I compensate the people working on those areas for me well because I want them to feel as if I honor their time and work. We honor someone's genius by paying them for it. Team building in this way should be part of your business plan and should be in line with the level of growth you want.

Since the beginning, I've had a CPA, a payroll service, a billing service, a credentialing service, an electronic medical records service, an IT guy, and administrative staff running the daily operations of SMPsychotherapy. Find ways to streamline your systems for invoicing, payroll, taxes, inventory, and other aspects of your business. Work with an attorney to ensure you're meeting all legal expectations and create policies for hiring and onboarding.

I hire therapists and psychiatric nurse practitioners and allow them to work in their areas of genius because that's the fastest route to success for the whole company. That isn't to say the people I hire or bring on board always work out. Sometimes people don't fit in with the mission and values of your business. Don't spend too much time worrying about that. The people who are meant to be part of your journey will stay. God will take care of the rest.

To develop your systems and support in your business plan, consider the following:

❖ What systems and support do you need to put into place?

❖ Who do you need to help you set up and run your business? (Administrative staff, attorney, CPA, business coach, etc.)

❖ What parts of running a business can you easily outsource so you can work in your area of genius?

❖ Which support should you hire first?

❖ How will you hire staff?

❖ What is your onboarding process?

❖ How will you handle letting staff members go when they aren't a good fit?

Chapter Takeaways

❖ You must develop and heal yourself because any areas of struggle will manifest in your business.

❖ With the right mindset, your business will have a strong foundation to expand and grow.

❖ 90-99% of your business success is spiritual—it's based on your mindset and willingness to expand.

❖ 1-10% of your business success is business strategy.

Self-Evaluation Prompts

❖ Identify one knowledge gap.

❖ What do you need to learn to advance toward your goals?

❖ What are you afraid of?

❖ Organize your new knowledge into usable steps. Organizing your knowledge will help eliminate fear.

❖ What support systems do you need to start or grow your business?

❖ What is the first step you will take today to move toward your goal?

Chapter 11

Mind, Body, Spirit

*An unbreakable life requires
a holistic approach to self-care.*

What defines you?"

That's the question I asked Alice once she entered our Zoom meeting. She tilted her head, wavy hair falling over one shoulder, and bit her lip.

"Who is Alice? How do you describe yourself?" I stopped, wanting her to fill the empty space.

"Well," she paused, "I'm a mother and a wife. I am a care-taker of my parents." Now she was on a roll. "I run a local cafe, and I'm an insurance company executive."

I listened, nodded, and recognized something I see in many of my therapy and coaching clients. Alice defined herself by the roles in her life that served others. She was useful and valuable because she cared for her children, was someone's wife, and was a dutiful daughter. Her identity tied into her full-time successful career, even though her heart pulled her to go full-time in her business.

What's wrong with that? All the roles Alice filled took everything she had and then some. There wasn't any space left for her to be Alice—a woman with goals and dreams. A woman with a purpose and vision.

Alice came to me overwhelmed, stressed, anxious, and unfulfilled. But why? Alice, like many women, made decisions based on what she thought women were supposed to do and be. She was dutiful; she was generous. She was a good woman. But Alice was exhausted—too exhausted to put energy into her dreams. What made Alice think her job was to serve others? What made her think herself unworthy of support or undeserving of living her dreams?

In our work together, we discovered that Alice was dis-connected from her true purpose and the dreams she had dreamt of when she was a young girl. That girl's dream was to be a business owner and her own boss and create job opportunities for marginalized women. She traded her dreams for her parents' dreams and societal expectations of working in corporate America. She gave up dreaming and instead accepted the security of savings, insurance, and a retirement plan. She learned from her parents and society to do what was "secure," but she is far from feeling secure doing work that does not align with her true purpose and dreams.

She wanted to make her parents and those around her proud, but to do so, she sacrificed too much. Alice lived her life the way she thought she should. She paid attention to the needs of others, put herself last, and cared for her community. She didn't ask for help because asking others to assist her was weak and selfish. Other people deserved support more than she did. Alice's dreams and life were on hold.

But if we dive deeper, we discover that Alice was the creator of her own situation. Sure, societal expectations for women and ideas about what made women valuable caused her to fall deeper into a world where her lives were on hold. But the decision to place others' needs above her own and not delegate tasks or seek support were decisions Alice made. I'm not saying Alice chose to live a life devoid of satisfaction—I'm saying that if Alice chose not to chase her dreams, she could also choose to chase them with abandon. She could reconnect with that purpose she felt as a young person and build a life that fulfilled her. She already knew how to work hard—we just needed to channel that energy and effort into the passion she felt for helping marginalized women and building her own business.

Alice felt incapable of achieving balance in her life. How could she balance life, career, motherhood, and family relationships and still have time to care for her mind, body, and spirit? The truth I taught Alice, and that I attempt to teach all my clients with similar struggles, is that balance is a myth. Balance assumes there is a way to give equal time to all the important areas of your life. Balance assumes you're willing to give up pieces of the puzzle that throw off balance. Balance should never be the goal. The goal is alignment.

How do we achieve alignment? We rework our lives, so all our desires feed into our purpose and our passion. Our purpose must guide the partners we choose, how we love our people, how we parent our children, the work we do, and the communities we serve. You will always achieve your dreams when you align with your values, purpose, and desires. What's more, life becomes more fulfilling when you work in alignment. You don't have to sacrifice yourself or care for those you love. Alignment allows you to care for yourself so you're better able to give to others. Alignment is possible, but balance is not. My work with Alice focused on creating alignment, not on finding balance.

When you work in alignment with your purpose, it becomes easy to make decisions because you choose anything that helps move you toward your purpose of impacting lives and creating a legacy to support you and your children. To find a way toward alignment, you must determine where the belief about balance came from.

Where did you learn that balance was important and that balance was possible?

How is the belief in balance supporting or helping you in your quest for success? Is it helping you? Is it causing additional stress? Is it helping you achieve your dreams?

If believing in balance is not supporting your desire to build your business and achieve your dreams, it's time to uproot the belief. I recommend replacing the belief in balance with a belief in alignment. You can find a way to align your purpose with everything you do and everyone you love if you include yourself in the equation and work within your passion and purpose. You need to be strong, healthy, and full to give energy to your purpose. You also need the confidence and energy to work within that space. The energy and confidence require a new belief system and a reorganization of your life. You'll need to care for yourself the way you care for others. You'll need to define what you're working toward and design a life that supports it.

Much of this process requires reconnection with our spiritual selves. Your creator made you for a purpose. Your creator loves you. A huge component of doing your part means loving yourself enough to create your dream life. You are an unbreakable woman creating an unbreakable life. An unbreakable life requires a holistic approach to self-care.

When I began working with Alice, her commitments exceeded the number of weekly hours. She ran her own business, worked full time, volunteered in her community, invested in her marriage, had three children to care for, and was the primary caretaker for her aging parents. This led to overwhelming stress and anxiety and could have caused her to throw her entrepreneurial dreams out the window. So many women have dreams and allow the pressures of life to break them down.

"How do you feel in your life now, Alice?" I asked in an early session.

"Well, I love my family," Alice began, then paused. Tears welled in her eyes. "But mostly, I feel run-down and used up. I am always running around from place to place, and it seems like my to-do list only gets longer. I'm stressed all the time, and that causes me to snap at people I care about. And I want to spend more time at home with my husband and kids, but there's just so much to do with work, and my business, and then the community stuff. I guess I just don't know where to find more time for my family, let alone for myself."

Like so many women, Alice spent all her time being busy, but felt unfulfilled. My goal was to help Alice become an unbreakable woman. Alice's tendency to take on the burden of caring for others came from a good place—the desire to help and support. But she was working with an empty tank. She didn't delegate tasks to family and friends. She said yes to additional work even when she wanted to say no. A self-diagnosed people-pleaser, Alice felt that help and support were available to others, but if she asked for it, she was weak and selfish.

Does this sound familiar? The archetype of the selfless woman as the ideal causes so many women to let go of their dreams for more. Remember when I asked Alice who she was? All that described her were her roles. That is not an unbreakable life. An unbreakable woman knows she is worthy of time, support, and energy to chase her dreams. An unbreakable woman finds her tribe.

To guide Alice, I asked her the following questions:

❖ How do you want to feel instead?

❖ If you were working in alignment with your purpose in all areas of your life, how would you feel?

❖ What would you think if you were working in alignment with your purpose?

❖ How would you behave?

❖ What results would you experience if all things were aligned in your life?

Our thoughts become our feelings, and our feelings influence our behaviors. If we think we don't deserve to ask for help, hire a coach, or work toward our dreams, we will feel guilty for wanting to. If we feel guilt for our desires, we will not act. Our subconscious mind will use those feelings of guilt and shame to keep us rooted in our current situation. We will stay frozen in a space where busy fills our time and discontent fills our hearts. That's a dirty chair. Getting out of a dirty chair requires you to shift your thinking and perceptions of yourself, those around you, and the world. You rewire your subconscious mind when your mindset aligns with your dreams. You'll disempower the thoughts and feelings that keep you stuck and infuse thoughts and feelings that leave you energized.

There is a notion out there that self-care is manicures, massages, and expensive vacations. Let's be clear—those self-care methods are amazing but miss the point. True self-care moves you toward your purpose, realigns you to your path when you feel disconnected, and reminds you you are worthy of love, care, and support. To shift your mindset so you can care for yourself and create a Queendom worthy of your God-given talents, you must know what you truly desire, then make a plan and live in action mode. Because everything you need you already have. You are alive.

Understand What You Truly Desire

We often have divided minds. One part knows what we want out of life, and the other has doubts and worries that keep us from acting. Alice struggled with stating her goals and desires because she thought God's desire for her life was separate from hers. The reality is that God is your co-creator and lives inside you. The voice you hear saying, "there's got to be more to life than this," or "if only I could find a way to make my hobby a career," is the voice of God guiding you toward your purpose. The first step to learning to care for yourself and your dream is to identify exactly your true dream and describe it in detail.

To identify your true purpose and passion, start by finding a way to get quiet and tune into that little voice your fears and anxieties usually silence. Tell that fear to stay quiet so you can listen. I do this through meditation and journaling, but I have clients who take a walk in nature to reconnect to their inner voice—the guidance of their co-creator. Find the space where you can get quiet enough to hear that whispered dream.

Maybe your dream is to write a novel. Maybe you dream of creating a successful personal care brand. Maybe you want to design clothing that fits real bodies. Maybe you want to open a private therapy practice. Whatever your dream is, writing it down and learning to say it aloud will empower you to take the next step. If you struggle with identifying what you want, a therapist, life coach, or business coach can give you the support you need to find alignment in your mind. Start saying your dream aloud, writing it in your journal, and sharing it with people worthy of hearing it. Eliminating that duality—the opposing forces pushing you toward while also pulling you away from your dream—will make the next steps easier.

Make a Plan

Once you've identified your dream, you'll need to spend time formulating a plan for identifying what sort of self-care you need. How will you support yourself in chasing this dream you finally acknowledged? First, find the thoughts, feelings, and behavior patterns that had you stuck in an unfulfilled life. Do a self-evaluation and ask yourself what is not serving you and what is. Create a regular self-care practice that supports your physical, emotional, spiritual, and intellectual needs. When you properly care for yourself, you can build a business, care for loved ones, and increase your impact on the world. Do you need time each day for journaling and meditation? Do you need to take a walk each day and think about the strategy for your business? Do you need to spend time away from work and connect with family and friends? The table below lists things to consider as regular components of your self-care practice for each category. Choose some practices from each category and make them a regular part of your life so you can avoid the black hole of fear, guilt, and anxiety that render you unable to build your unbreakable life.

	Physical	Emotional	Spiritual	Intellectual
Get additional rest	X	X		X
Visit a church or synagogue			X	
Call or visit a friend		X	X	
Spend time with your children		X	X	
Exercise-: walk, gym	X	X		
Read -self-development or pleasure		X	X	X
Cook a delicious, healthy meal	X	X		
Spend time with your partner	X	X	X	
Prayer/ meditation		X	X	
Hike	X	X	X	
Listen to a podcast or online course		X	X	X

Get a massage or visit a spa	X	X	X	
Talk with a mentor		X		X
Watch a movie	X	X	X	X
Take a dance class	X	X		X
Other self-care practices *Hair* *Nails* *Massage* *Facials* *Vacations* *Dates nights* *Visit a friend*	X	X		

This self-care plan is not written in stone. It's more like a GPS. If you're on a road trip to a beach house for a two-week vacation and hit traffic or some other obstacle, you use your GPS to find an alternate route. You don't give up on your destination. Your self-care plan should include methods to help you reconnect with your purpose when the old doubts creep up.

There are days I wake up and bound out of bed, drape myself in the cloth of success, and behave like the unbreakable boss woman I am. There are other days, though, when I wake feeling weighed down and incapable of dream-building. On those days, I know I am grieving or in pain and need to take time to detour before returning to my path. If I don't take the time to work through those feelings, I will sit in them longer and make little forward progress. Giving myself the compassion to work through difficult times is self-care.

This happened most recently during the week of Thanksgiving. While my family prepared to feast together, I found myself exhausted, in physical pain, and generally low. I took time to journal and realized I was sitting in my dirty chair of grief about losing Jean Carlos. His death shook me, and occasionally, as it did at Thanksgiving, it overwhelmed me again. I knew I needed to make a plan to rise out of that dirty chair so I could get back to building my Queendom. I continued journaling and made a plan to support myself. Honoring my needs at that moment meant giving myself a weekend of extra rest, large mugs of tea, time with my family, watching movies, meditation, and nourishing food. I threw in a spa visit as well for good measure. I gave myself the gift of rest to return to building my legacy on Monday morning.

Sometimes, when these negative emotions strike, we cannot stop our lives for a four-day weekend. Perhaps you're grieving the loss of a relationship but still need to show up and be present at work. Maybe you're mourning the loss of a loved one while caring for children too young to understand your need for time and personal space. You may not be able to have all you need to recover at once, but you can certainly plan for bits of self-care to help you reconnect to your true purpose.

Try a slight schedule modification and nap while your toddler sleeps instead of worrying about the laundry. You may not be able to take a long, hot bath, but can you find fifteen minutes? You can't take a whole weekend off of family and work responsibilities, but can you find a few hours to give yourself time to read a book with a cup of coffee?

Don't let perfection be the enemy of progress in your self-care routines. Sure, we'd all love to rush off to the spa every time we struggle, but that's not how life works. Do better care for yourself this year than you did last year. Progress will breed more progress. Soon, you'll reframe those thoughts that you don't deserve support and time to chase your dreams. You'll begin to think about what your body, mind, and spirit need to be healthy and give it to yourself as a friend. The guilt over wanting more for your life will fade, and you'll move toward your purpose.

Live in Action Mode

Moving toward your goals and making the things you want part of your reality motivates you to do more. True self-care involves not only things that support your mental and emotional health. Self-care means honoring your dreams and goals with intentional action. You may not have the time to build your dream for hours every day—Alice certainly didn't when we started working together. But, by keeping your mindset on forward motion and success, carving out the time for the building where you can, and taking in information that renews your mind, fortifies your spirit, and heals your body, you will build your unbreakable life.

For Alice, action mode meant healing the subconscious thoughts and patterns that kept her in a self-denial mindset. Her action plan included appointments with a therapist and coach to ensure she continued working to replace old, unhelpful thought patterns with new ones. She worked on affirmations to ensure those thoughts were repeated in her mind throughout her days. Repeated things get remembered—that's why our old beliefs are ingrained. To make a growth mindset intent on success part of who you are, you must repeat the thoughts until they form a new belief system.

Being in action mode means dealing with negative emotions and thoughts of unworthiness. Dealing with them does not mean ignoring them. Instead, I worked with Alice to identify the feelings that came up when she had thoughts about how she shouldn't be taking care of herself, canceling her obligations in the community, and deciding to spend time with her family instead of working all the time. Those feelings come from thought processes that say women must be givers and be selfless. God does not want you to be selfless. He would never ask you to give up pieces of what makes you the magnificent, creative being you are. God wants you to hold onto yourself, nourish yourself, love yourself, and use your gifts to create a beautiful life here on earth. Any thoughts to the contrary will negatively impact how you show up in your business. In action mode, we identify the feelings, find the root cause, and then consciously release that thought and replace it with a new one worthy of the dream we're building.

Another part of action mode for Alice was caring for her body. She already produced most of the food she ate on her family farm. She knew healthy eating was vital to building a successful life. But, she often felt guilty for taking time to herself for exercise or seeing specialists to help with pain and fatigue. We created an action plan, including regular chiropractor visits and cranial sacral therapy to help her stay centered and keep her body working well. When Alice struggled with anxiety about life, family, dreams, or business decisions, she needed to walk her property or take a hike with her dogs. Alice began to see that the more she cared for her physical body, the more she felt connected to her purpose and creator.

Taking care of your body doesn't require massive changes, or an expensive personal trainer, though you can certainly include those things if you wish. For diet changes, try including more fruits and vegetables—the vitamins and minerals will help fuel your body and keep you feeling your best. Find exercise classes you enjoy, like Zumba or yoga, or just go for a walk. Make regular appointments with your doctor and get your physical each year.

The third part of the action mode requires you to say no to practices that don't serve your purpose. Often, this means establishing new, healthier boundaries with friends, loved ones, employers, and your community. For Alice, this meant saying no to many of the community organizations she was part of. She thought being a good woman required her to give selflessly until there wasn't much left of her. Helping others is valuable, and if it's aligned with your purpose can help you build an unbreakable life. If, however, helping others leaves you depleted or takes away from activities more closely connected to your purpose, they need to go. Every time you say yes to someone else, you're saying no to yourself. A yes to running the PTA may be a no to the time with your family you care about. A yes to doing work without pay may be a no to a lucrative opportunity that can help you and your family financially. Say yes only when it doesn't derail you from your purpose and your dreams.

When Alice and I began our work together, she had difficulty visualizing herself as a woman who was supported in her dreams. She spent so much time and energy giving to others there was no energy left to fuel her purpose. I engaged her in recovering and embracing the importance of self-care by using the Queen archetype I've used throughout this book. Building a Queendom requires you to be supported and loved. First, you must love yourself and engage in enough self-care to deem yourself worthy of support to achieve your dreams. Then, you must understand that a Queen never works alone. Now, Alice is building her Queendom. She's invited her family and friends to support her dream. Alice now delegates household tasks and trusts that the people around her will step up. Alice put together a self-care practice that keeps her connected to her purpose and gives her the energy she needs to chase her dreams. She's extending that learning to her daughter and teaching her to honor her true self. Alice also learned to create and enforce better boundaries by always ending appointments on time, adjusting her schedule to allow for family time, and hiring support for her business.

When you're a Queen building your Queendom, you'll need to define yourself based on your standards, not society's. Queens are defined by their purpose and their dreams, not by the roles they fill. You may be a mother, a wife, a nurse, a teacher, or a therapist. You may be a business owner and an author. None of those roles define you. You are a Queen. You are a visionary. You are constantly growing and changing. The rest of how you define yourself is between you and your co-creator. You are good enough, and you deserve all you desire because you are. No explanation is required.

Queens never work in isolation, and they don't work depleted. They work to fill themselves with practices to support their mind, body, and spirit. Queens treat self-care as part of their job—because it absolutely is. Queens seek support when they need it. They seek support for their mental, emotional, spiritual, and physical health from loved ones, mentors, and therapists. They seek out opportunities for deep introspection so they can remain connected to their co-creator and to their purpose. I know you can do all this because you're already a Queen. You're a Queen because your Creator bestowed gifts upon you that you can use to create a huge impact in this world. You can change lives and build the life you want. I can't wait to see the Queendom you create and witness who you become.

Chapter Takeaways

❖ Self-care is a form of self-love. It is not selfish.

❖ Caring for everyone else from a place of emptiness leads to unhealthy relationships.

❖ Develop a self-care practice that supports your mission, vision, and dreams.

❖ When you live in your purpose and serve from a place of fulfillment, you maximize your impact on the world.

Self-Evaluation Prompts

❖ Identify a situation as a young child, teen, or young woman that taught you about self-care and what it means for women.

❖ Identify the women around you who taught you about self-care or the lack of self-care.

❖ What did you learn from what other women said and did or didn't do about their self-care?

❖ Identify a new belief system around the value of self-care and how you want your self-care practices to support you and your business or career.

❖ Create a holistic self-care plan that supports your dreams, goals, and purpose.

Conclusion

How to Keep Building Your Dream

You've built momentum through the self-evaluation prompts in this book. You've connected with the stories and found areas where you want to grow. Maybe you've discovered a dream you didn't realize existed or reconnected to a goal. As you close this book, I implore you not to stop dreaming. Keep the momentum going.

Do the work. Continue to heal the wounds of grief, loss, and trauma. Therapy, journaling, meditation, and all the other strategies I urged you to use throughout this book will be your greatest companions as you work through the difficult parts of life that caused you to forget to dream in the first place.

Remember that mindset work never ends. Even the most successful entrepreneurs must continuously remind themselves they are worthy of investment, growth, love, and care. Continue that work through journaling, affirmations, reading, and speaking with others who can help lift you.

Plan for success, and plan to change your plan. You will encounter roadblocks, but if you have a plan guided by purpose and open to detours, you will always reach your destination.

Be open to change. Work to continuously evaluate your progress, missteps, and successes and make shifts in your plan. Evaluate your business, mindset, and goals regularly and adjust the course as needed.

Stay in action mode. Even a small action in the right direction is helpful. You may not be able to take massive, inspired action every day. Do something anyway.

Find support because you are a Queen, and a Queen never works alone. Seek mentors, therapists, and coaches to support you emotionally while pushing you in the ways you need. Rely on friends and family when you hit adversity.

Rest, recover, and care for yourself. A Queen can only give to others when she is well cared for and fully loved. You don't need anyone else to take care of your needs. Find the things that fill your cup and do them regularly. Tune into your emotions and rest when needed. A well-rested and well-loved Queen can build any dream.

Oh, and if you didn't download that workbook I linked in the introduction, here is your reminder. Download the workbook, work through the prompts, and get started on your Queendom. I can't wait to celebrate your success.

Here's the link:

go.becomeunbreakablebook.com/workbook

The Next Steps

I've encouraged you to keep the momentum you built while reading *Unbreakable* and engaging with the self-evaluation prompts. Here are some concrete steps you can take to ensure you keep growing, stay connected with your purpose, and build your unbreakable life.

❖ **Download your self-care template.** I created this so you can make your holistic, unbreakable self-care practice that will support you in creating the life of your dreams.

❖ **Get the *Unbreakable Journal*.** After writing Unbreakable, I felt called by my creator to do more for my readers. I created a beautiful journal for you to use to deepen your self-evaluation process and learn more about your purpose and the life God created you to live. The full-color journal is available now.

❖ **UNBREAKABLE - THE COURSE!**

Register for Unbreakable, the online course that will teach you how to align your vision with your purpose so you can create an unbreakable business, life, and career.

The first round of Unbreakable will be a live teaching experience with me. After that, students will have access to all recordings, including question-and-answer sessions.

This six-week course includes:

- ❖ Six weekly class sessions

- ❖ Two group coaching sessions with Soribel.

- ❖ A Facebook community to share struggles and successes and gain support.

- ❖ A membership site with course materials and bonuses.

The course content will be a deeper dive into the concepts in *Unbreakable*, including:

- ❖ The Queendom Architect - how alignment with your purpose can build a legacy.

- ❖ Self-evaluation and analysis - become aware of where you are by activating your inner GPS. Find paths to growth and healing.

- ❖ Personal development - reclaiming your power and voice, finding your support system, and investing in yourself!

- ❖ Develop your holistic, unbreakable self-care practice.

- ❖ Planning for success - including mindset and practical career tips and strategies for starting your own unbreakable business.

- ❖ And so much more!

❖ Schedule a Consultation Call

I offer individual business and career coaching services for women who want more in-depth guidance as they build an unbreakable life. Apply to join my exclusive private coaching programs here.

Connect with Soribel Martinez

SMPsychotherapy & Counseling Services
https://psychotherapyandcounselingservices.com/

Facebook:
https://www.facebook.com/SoribelMartinezLCSW

Instagram:
https://www.instagram.com/smpsychotherapy/

https://www.instagram.com/xoxoSoribel

LinkedIn:
https://www.linkedin.com/in/soribelmartinez/

Business Coaching, Consulting & Mentoring
https://www.soribelmartinez.com

Hire Soribel Martinez for Your Next Conference, Training or Speaking Event

Did you Love *Unbreakable* and can't wait for more inspiration? Soribel is an authority on mental health, business, and personal development, but her presentations come across as inspirational and energetic instead of dry and academic. Whether she's presenting about personal development, mental health, or building a business, Soribel's unique voice and perspective on the intersection of life and business will leave listeners encouraged to move forward and take inspired, massive action toward their dreams.

Soribel Martinez, LCSW, is available to speak at your next event about

❖ **Unbreakable Leadership**: Learn about inspired leadership and how it impacts the world. What is a leadership mindset and how can we develop one that aligns with our purpose, vision, and mission? How to develop an Unbreakable Leadership Mindset

- ❖ **How to Build an Unbreakable Business:** Business Development for Health and Mental Health professionals in Private Practice: Learn Soribel's proven system, the 8 Pillars of Private Practice to build and scale your business. Find out how you can create a private practice that supports your vision *and* revenue goals.

- ❖ **Unbreakable Personal Development:** Navigate adversity, eliminate self-doubt, learn to love yourself well, and surround yourself with others who believe in your dreams. Stop letting life happen to you and create the life you were meant to live. How to build an Unbreakable life

- ❖ **Unbreakable Professional Development:** This program guides participants to create the career they want regardless of their field. Participants will be inspired to take massive action, learn to handle conflict, stand up for what they want, and ask for what they deserve.

"At my Una-apologetically me women's retreat, Ms. Martinez's passion for helping women was clear. She possesses a wealth of knowledge. Attendees come away with incredible takeaways every time she speaks."

Mary Ann Francis LMFT
Founder of Una-pologetically

For more information and to book a consultation, visit this link:

https://soribelmartinez.com/media

About the Author

Soribel Martinez, Licensed Clinical Psychotherapist is a visionary. She believes in a world where women create legacies and understand they are Queens who can build their own Queendom with the right tools, support, and mindset. Soribel believes women are not defined by their roles, but by the purpose they were born to fulfill. Her purpose is to help women create lives and legacies they're proud of while learning to love themselves just as they were created.

Soribel was born in the Dominican Republic and immigrated to the United States when she was twelve years old. She holds bachelor's degrees in psychology and biology from Post University and completed two years of medical school at SABA School of Medicine before deciding mental health care was her true calling. She achieved a master's degree in psychology and social work, and then returned for her MBA because she always dreamed of running her own business. A believer in lifelong learning, Soribel is currently a Doctor of Social Work candidate at Walden University.

Soribel accomplishes her purpose by working as a psychotherapist and business coach and consultant while running a group private therapy practice. She developed the principles of the Million Dollar Private Practice to build and scale SMPyschotherapy and Counseling Services into the dynamic practice it is today. SMPsychotherapy employs over twenty-five licensed mental health therapists and two psychiatric mental health nurse practitioners, as well as administrative staff. Soribel's group practice serves over eleven thousand clients. Her coaching programs help other women build and scale their own businesses and create their dream life.

Soribel expanded her purpose to help women build their dreams by founding JC's Precious Minds Foundation in 2021 to honor the memory of her son, Jean-Carlos. Soribel believes in honoring the women and family members who came before her and paved the path to her success. She believes in honoring herself by answering the call for her purpose, and she seeks to honor the future generation by creating a legacy and a blueprint for growth and success.

In addition to being a CEO, and the founder of a nonprofit, Soribel is a mother, a speaker, a storyteller, an adjunct professor of psychology at Post University, a member of the Post University's Malcolm Baldrige School of Business-Management Advisory Board. She's a bestselling author and a concierge sex therapist, but she wants to remind her readers that none of those roles define her or establish her worth.

Accomplishments and titles do not determine how much you love yourself, or how much you're supported by your creator. Soribel is worthy because she is, just as you are worthy because you are. Soribel lives in Connecticut with her mother and son, John Anthony. She spends her free time with family, traveling around the world, reading, and learning as much as she can. Soribel wrote this book to inspire you to heal, transform, and build the life you were created to live.

JC's Precious Minds Foundation

JC's Precious Minds Foundation seeks to help single mothers of children with disabilities with financial and educational resources. Soribel began the foundation to honor the memory of her son, Jean-Carlos, who was stillborn at 36 weeks. Grief is like the ocean, with small waves that cause you to catch your breath, and large waves that threaten to knock you over. The ocean is powerful, and so is grief. If you channel it, you can use it to create a greater impact in the world than you dreamed possible.

JC's Precious Minds Foundation provides financial resources, housing, food, clothing, special education, testing services, occupational, physical, and speech therapy, psychological services, and extracurricular activities to special needs children of single mothers in the Dominican Republic. In addition to helping children reach their potential, the foundation assists single mothers with returning to school, and/or starting their own business. Every child and every woman deserve the support necessary to thrive.

In December 2022 the foundation received its first donation of $150,000. The foundation began with four families and currently serves ten with plans to further expand.

JC's Precious Mind Foundation Recipient

"First and foremost, we want to express our gratitude to this wonderful initiative, JC's Precious Mind Foundation, which has impacted the lives of every member of this family.

I experienced a sense of the end of the world when Ramses was diagnosed with autism. With him, it was nearly impossible to leave the house because I was so worried about his future that I sobbed nonstop for a while. Then, in 2021, I obtained assistance from JC's Precious Mind Foundation, who were like angels sent by God. Since that time, my family's dynamic has totally changed.

Since Ramses began taking classes, receiving therapy, and receiving food, we have been able to witness his progress to the extent that our son Ramses is no longer the same as he was a year ago. We are moved by every new word he says, every new food he requests and tries, and by every new action he takes. Everything I once imagined my son could do, he has accomplished thanks to the collaboration and support of JC's Precious Mind Foundation. We can only say THANK YOU because without your assistance, who knows where we would be."

Mercedes Alejandrina Tavarez
Mother of Ramsés, a 6-Year-Old Boy

Green Heart Living Press publishes inspirational books and stories of transformation, making the world a more loving and peaceful place, one book at a time. You can meet Green Heart authors on the Green Heart Living YouTube channel and the Green Heart Living Podcast.

www.greenheartliving.com

Made in the USA
Middletown, DE
21 May 2023

30820749R00099